indian
heritage hotels

indian
heritage hotels
legacy of splendour

Atithi Devo Bhava
Guest is God
—Rig Veda

anuradha kapoor

Lustre Press
Roli Books

introduction
restoring majesty

The 'past' is very much a part of the here and now in India. What makes Indian civilization, along with China's, special is that it has continued in an unbroken continuum from the early ancient times right up till the present day. History, tradition and cultural heritage are not mothballed relics consigned to museums and inner recesses of the people's collective memory, only to be dusted and displayed periodically. They are an integral and organic part of her people's everyday life.

It is in this spirit that many of India's numerous forts, palaces, havelis and colonial mansions have been rescued from oblivion and converted into fine heritage properties, open to the traveller looking for an authentic cultural experience.

The age of mass tourism is here and there is no dearth of hotels and accommodations practically anywhere in the globe for someone looking to travel and sightsee. The near universal availability of boarding and lodging, with options ranging from budget to super luxury, would have been considered unlikely, if not impossible, not too long ago. But, like many other gifts of the modern age, it is often seen as a mixed blessing. There is often a trade-off between the touch of authentic local flavour and uniqueness of experience on the one hand, and time, comfort and convenience on the other. Draw the curtains or blinds in a luxury hotel room and, very often, it will be a challenge to guess where you are—New York or New Delhi, Bangkok or Berlin, Cairo or Sydney!

Which is why the concept of heritage hotels has been steadily gaining in popularity with many discerning travellers worldwide. And India, which is fast emerging as a popular tourist destination internationally, has many charming heritage properties. These mostly consist of old palaces, hilltop forts, hunting lodges and colonial bungalows—some dating back centuries—which not only showcase India's traditions and customs, but also bring alive the flavour, ambience and feel of her rich past. Staying in a heritage hotel can add to the guest's experience of a place in many ways, whether she is visiting a place of historical or religious significance, a wildlife sanctuary or an eco-tourism destination.

Typically, these hotels tend to be small and are run on a different, more personal, scale as compared to the modern, metropolitan luxury hotels. Spare and elegant, or, rich, grand and regal—heritage properties now dot all corners of India's vast, subcontinental expanse. And in keeping with India's rich and varied traditions which go back deep in antiquity, they vary widely in their architecture, interiors and cultural offerings.

The forts and palaces could range from purely functional to unabashedly ornamental.

Surrounded by a moat, turreted and having walls as thick as seventeen feet, citadels like the Neemrana Fort near Delhi and the Bassi Fort in Chittorgarh were designed with one

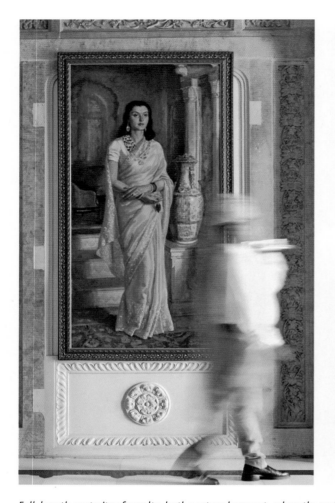

Full-length portraits of royalty, both past and present, adorn the walls of Rambagh Palace. Below: *Sawai Man Singh II of Jaipur.*

purpose in mind—to keep out invaders. Their grand, austere facades can be contrasted to the bright, graceful exteriors of the Rambagh Palace in Jaipur, the Lalitha Mahal Palace in Mysore and the Lallgarh Palace in Bikaner. The marble or pink-sandstone palaces were often dedicated to unabashed display of wealth and luxury, their walls inlaid with silver and jade, and adorned with pietra dura (inlay) patterns using precious stones like turquoise and garnet. The rooms and halls within are exquisitely decorated with period furnishings—Belgian mirrors, crystal chandeliers, and beautiful, often rare, paintings.

A sanctuary from bland modernity where taste and refinement are not necessarily a priority, heritage hotels nonetheless offer all the modern conveniences, coming equipped with facilities like luxurious spas that offer Ayurvedic and wellness treatments, gyms and swimming pools.

Many of India's surviving forts and palaces were built during the 16th through the 18th century, when the country was divided into many provinces and kingdoms, each under a local ruler. The Mughal emperors in Delhi ruled as the overall sovereigns of the greater part of the

The Durbar thrones in Jaipur, c. 1875.

subcontinent, their power and influence waxing and waning with the vicissitudes of time.

Among the more colourful and flamboyant rulers were the Rajputs—inhabiting the region to the southwest of Delhi, which largely consists of the great Thar desert, and is now part of the state of Rajasthan. They were known for the strong sense of pride they took in their traditions and way of life, imbued as it was with the knightly ideals of valour, honour and chivalry.

The British ruled over India in the 19th and 20th century and the Indian princes and kings were no longer required to maintain huge armies and wage ruinous wars. This freed up a lot of resources and much of it was channelled into building lavish, elaborate palaces. Another distinct architectural style

that emerged in 19th-century India was what is popularly known as the Indo-Saracenic style—a fusion of the Indo-Islamic and European architecture. New palaces, modelled on the European style, started replacing the older ones and reflected the newly acquired tastes of the maharajas.

There was also, in the 19th century, a resurgence of a vibrant Rajput style of architecture, which gave a much-needed impetus to local craftsmen, especially in the states of Jodhpur, Bikaner and Jaipur. The British architect Samuel Swinton Jacob is credited with the revival of the Rajput style. Palaces designed by him make abundant use of traditional features such as *jalis* (filigreed screens), *jharokas* (ornate windows), *chattris* (cupolas), cusped arches and bangle roofs. The 'Neo-Rajput' style took a firm hold on the Indian maharaja's imagination. The result may sometimes look idiosyncratic, but has its own distinct charm. The art deco style of architecture became prominent during the first half of the 20th century. India gained independence in 1947 and the princely states were absorbed into the Indian union. Bereft of their kingdoms, the maharajas and maharanis had to severely curtail their extravagances. Later, in 1971, their privy purses—generous annual remittances by the state that were guaranteed by the law—were also withdrawn. The maintenance of huge palaces, of which many royal families had at least two or three, became financially untenable. Some sold their properties and family heirlooms so that they could carry on, while some were forced to abandon their forts and palaces, which fell prey to neglect and decay. Some of the more enterprising ones, though, converted their properties into hotels.

Here again, the descendents of the proud and hardy Rajput princes took the pioneering role, showing remarkable agility and adaptability in adjusting with the changing times. One such pioneer was Maharaja Man Singh of Jaipur, an impetuous but practical man who decided in 1957 that Jaipur, the capital of the state of Rajasthan needed a hotel. He relinquished his residence, the sprawling Rambagh Palace where he stayed with his three wives, their children and hundreds of retainers. In December 1957, the Rambagh Palace became India's first palace hotel and opened its doors to Count Artaza, the Spanish ambassador to India. Today, it remains one of the finest luxury heritage hotels in India.

Set in a 47-acre garden, Rambagh Palace was first built in the 1800s, and subsequently expanded many times, the last expansion being in the 1930s when Man Singh married the beautiful Gayatri Devi. Atypically for her time and milieu, Gayatri Devi shot tigers, rode horses, drove cars, wore slacks and summered with film stars on the Riviera. Now in her eighties, she lives in a separate residence in the city, but can occasionally be seen having dinner with guests at the Rambagh hotel.

With over a hundred heritage hotels, Rajasthan is the logical starting point for a tour of India's palace hotels.

The wedding procession of Prince Karni Singh of Bikaner in the Junagarh Fort.

Attention to detail and authenticity is the hallmark of excellence, be it in the palaces of the past or heritage properties of today.

Legend has it that it is here that the first prince, born of the Sun, touched the Earth and started the royal lineage of Rajput warriors. It is in this desert region—where caravans from Kashmir, China and Persia exchanged fruit, opium, silks and arms; where many a conqueror clashed with the Rajputs; where the rich folk traditions are still vibrant and alive—that many forts, palaces and traditional havelis (mansions) can be found.

The heritage properties have mostly been restored to their original grandeur and special attention is given to their maintenance and conservation. There is a genuine attempt to provide a glimpse into a way of life that has long since lapsed and to recreate the vanished ambience. Much of the charm of these heritage hotels is in the individual attention and personalized service. Families, often in residence for many decades, welcome visitors as they would guests to their own homes. Naturally, each ancestral heritage property tends to be uniquely different, reflecting its own history, tradition

Fine craftsmanship at display in things small and big.

and culture. On many occasions, a visit to heritage hotels also provides a window into life in rural India—its diverse cuisines, festivals and fairs, folk dances and music. Heritage destinations provide opportunities for adventure—like a camel or horse safari, or a jeep-ride through the forest or sand dunes—which are not only enjoyable but also add an extra dimension to the visitor's experience.

According to the Indian Heritage Hotels Association (IHHA), its membership has grown from just 51 hotels in 1991 to 154 in 2004. The actual number of heritage hotels is higher as some properties function independently, without being affiliated with the association. Among its members are well-known hotel chains like the ITC Welcomgroup which leads the pack with thirty-five heritage hotels under its WelcomHeritage banner, followed by Historic Resort Hotels (HRH) headed by Arvind Singh Mewar, scion of the royal family of Udaipur, which has twelve properties. In the past decade, the Neemrana group of hotels, promoted by Aman Nath and Francis Wacziarg has also emerged as a heritage hotel chain of great repute with eleven hotels in its portfolio.

While a greater number of heritage properties are situated in the northern and western part of the country (in the states of Rajasthan and Gujarat) there are many heritage hotels in the southern and eastern parts of India too. So, get ready to journey through some of India's best heritage properties in the pages that follow.

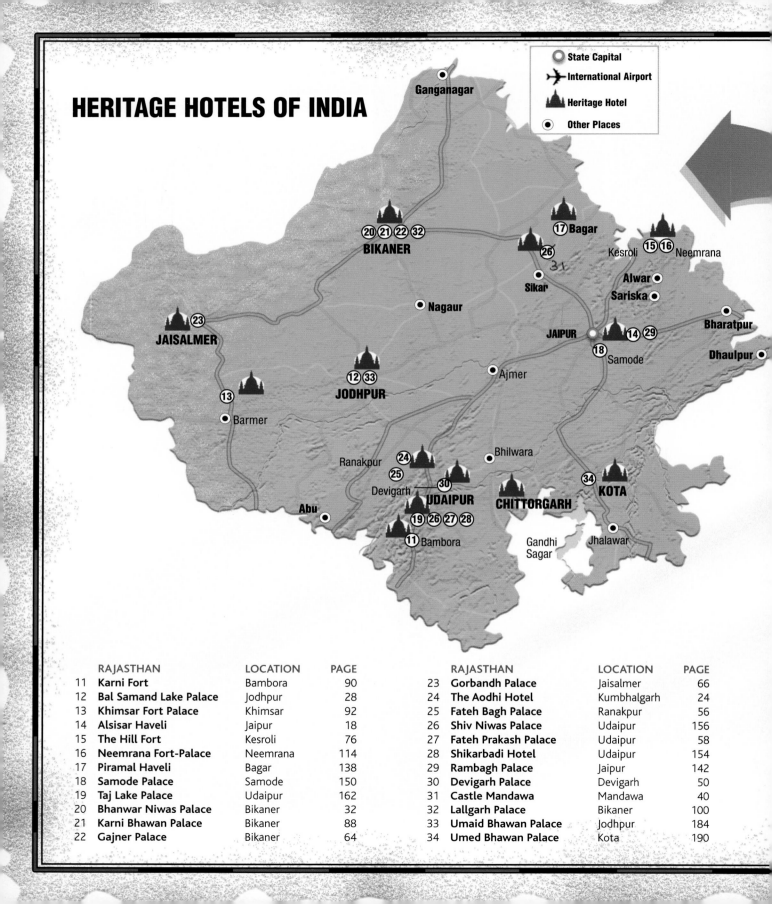

HERITAGE HOTELS OF INDIA

State Capital
International Airport
Heritage Hotel
Other Places

Ganganagar

⑳ ㉑ ㉒ ㉜
BIKANER

⑰ Bagar

㉖
31

Kesroli ⑮ ⑯ Neemrana

Sikar

Alwar

Sariska

Nagaur

JAIPUR

⑭ ㉙

Bharatpur

㉓
JAISALMER

⑬

⑫ ㉝
JODHPUR

Barmer

⑱ Samode

Dhaulpur

Ajmer

Ranakpur

㉔

㉕

Bhilwara

Devigarh ㉚

UDAIPUR

CHITTORGARH

㉞ **KOTA**

Abu

⑲ ㉖ ㉗ ㉘

⑪ Bambora

Gandhi
Sagar

Jhalawar

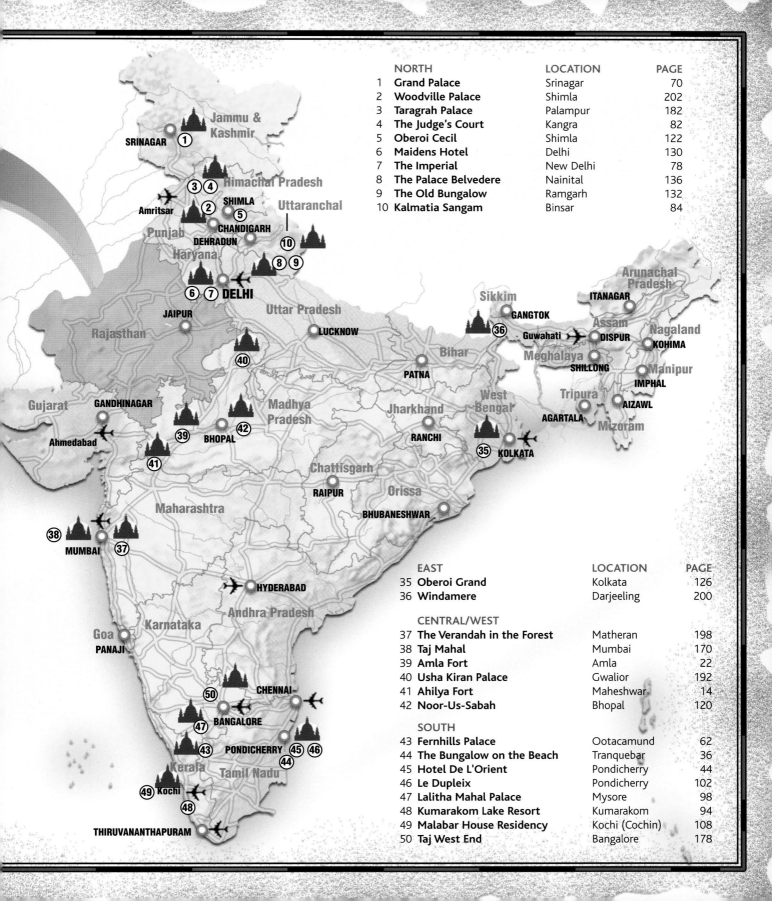

Location
Perched on the edge of a cliff, the massive walls of the Ahilya Fort in Maheshwar offer breathtaking views of the Narmada river and the ghats (riverbanks) immediately below.

Access
Airport: Indore – 91 km | **Railway Station:** Indore – 110 km | **International Airport:** Mumbai – 500 km
Driving Distance: From Bhopal – 276 km

ahilya fort
narmada's sentinel
Maheshwar, Madhya Pradesh

Email: info@ahilyafort.com

DYNASTY: Holkars • BUILT: 1766 • RENOVATION: ongoing since 2002
ARCHITECT (RENOVATION): Ravindra Gundu Rao and Associates
STYLE: Maratha Wada • CATEGORY: Mid Price

Linger over a gourmet meal prepared by a former prince, sip champagne on the ramparts of an ancient fort and watch the river-life unfold before you. If you want to do something more purposeful and energetic, go ahead and take a dip in the Narmada's cool and unpolluted waters and then set sail on a boat to Baneshwar Temple in the middle of the river.

Local legend has it that the Baneshwar Temple is the centre of the universe—the axis, which connects the centre of the earth and the Pole Star is believed to pass through it. The small town of Masheshwar, seemingly untouched by change, lies in central India and if you are looking for a place that is off the beaten track this is it. Here, you can spend days just unwinding, or weeks exploring the surrounding areas steeped in history.

Queen Ahilya Bai's Residence

While Maheshwar itself has a history that goes back at least 4,000 years, it was the Mughal emperor Akbar who first built the ramparts of the fort in 1601. Queen Ahilya Bai Holkar, the legendary Maratha ruler, commissioned the building of the fort as her residence in 1766. Couple of years ago, her descendent Shivaji Rao (Richard) Holkar converted the Ahilya Fort into a charming guest residence while ensuring that it is preserved and retains its traditional elegance. In fact, if Ahilya Bai were to look at it today she would find it practically unchanged, even two hundred and fifty years later.

Wada Architecture

The Ahilya Fort is a perfect example of the Wada style of Maratha architecture that came into existence during the reign of the Peshwas in the 18th century. The Wada structures were made using wooden pillars and the supporting beams were filled with lime, mud and bricks. A meticulous conservation programme, which began in 2002, has used traditional techniques and materials such as original lime mortar and recuperated wood from demolished period houses to reconstruct the damaged walls and foundations of the fort.

Ahilya Fort is essentially designed like a small housing complex; there are no more than two rooms in any one building, ensuring privacy and variety. Each room is unique, retaining its 18th–century flourishes, but has comfortable four-poster beds and modern plumbing.

Abounding in myths and legends, Ahilya Fort gives visitors an opportunity to veer off the tourist trail whilst still offering many things to see and do in Maheshwar. Within the fort there are delightful, lush courtyards and verandahs on different levels connected by stone pathways, making it a wonderful place to just wander around or explore the hidden terraces and turrets. Or one can spend hours gazing at the spectacular sights and sounds of the sacred river from the battlements or stroll alongside the riverside undisturbed by other tourists.

At the end of the day guests can dine on a traditional thali meal alfresco under the grand old trees on one of the terraces or in the Chamber of Winds, overlooking the Narmada river. Much of the food is organically grown on Ahilya Fort's nearby farm or sourced directly from where it is grown—be it a select tea garden in Darjeeling or a coffee plantation in Coorg.

Around Maheshwar

A must-do is a trip to the magnificent, abandoned city of Mandu just 60 kilometres away, a 15th-century marvel of early Islamic architecture set amongst forests and ravines at the edge of the Malwa plateau. The famed island of Omkareshwar and other temples dating back to hundreds of years are also just 50 kilometres upstream.

Ahilya Bai and the Holkars

Malhar Rao Holkar, the founder of the House of Holkars was born in 1693. His military acumen earned him the respect of the Peshwas of Pune and he was rewarded with the gift of territories comprising the Indore region. Malhar Rao was succeeded by his daughter-in-law Maharani Devi Ahilya Bai—one of the most able and extraordinary rulers of India. Sir John Malcolm, in his *Memoirs of Central India*, described the queen as a 'female without vanity... exercising in the more active and able manner, despotic power with sweet humanity...'

Ahilya Bai's cherished desire was to promote the prosperity of the region and its people. She was the rare Indian royalty who was deified in her lifetime. Though the brave Holkar queen planned and built Indore, she resided in Maheshwar at Ahilya Fort and it was only after her death that the state capital was shifted to Indore in 1811.

Location
Close to the walled city of Jaipur, Alsisar Haveli is a fine example of the traditional Rajasthani mansion, with its large courtyard and corridors with arched pillars, and surrounded by lush gardens.

Access
Airport: Jaipur – 12 km | **Railway Station:** Jaipur – 2 km | **International Airport:** New Delhi – 250 km

alsisar haveli

classic elegance

Jaipur, Rajasthan

Email: alsisar@alsisar.com

DYNASTY: Kachhawaha/Shekhawati Rajputs • BUILT: 1892
RENOVATION: 1994 • STYLE: Rajput & Mughal • CATEGORY: Budget

It is often said that if you turn a stone in Jaipur you will find an old haveli under it. Among the scores of havelis dotting the city, the Alsisar Haveli stands out and is one of the Pink City's best-kept secret. Even though it is located in the heart of Jaipur, its large garden distances you from the urban bustle and clatter.

Shekhawati City Residence

About five hundred years ago, Rao Shekhaji, a Kachhawaha Rajput and grandson of the Maharaja Udaikaran of Amber, founded the sub-clan popularly known as 'Shekhawat'. Though they moved to an area in the interiors of Rajasthan called Shekhawati, they kept their links with Jaipur. Alsisar Haveli was built in 1892 by members of this branch and became their city residence. Today, the descendants of the family have converted the old mansion into a modern hotel, while retaining the old furniture and frescoes on the walls.

Traditional Charms

Refurbished in 1994, the haveli incorporates a mix of the traditional Rajput and Mughal architecture. The large elevated platform that dominates the central area of the ground floor, once used by the men of the house only, is now open to all. Here guests can watch puppet shows and folk dances. The spacious lobby or Sheesh Mahal, inspired by the Amber Fort in Jaipur, opens into an inner courtyard that was used only by the ladies of the house till a century ago, but has now been converted into a lounge.

The mansion has thirty-six rooms with carved antique furniture, restored frescos, rug-covered floors and antique mirrors. The double-ceiling dining room has real gold inlay work on the walls, chandeliers and old paintings. The pièce de résistance at Alsisar is the pool—with glass mosaic floors and pavilions on four sides, reminiscent of the public step-wells where villagers would congregate, do their chores and exchange gossip.

In and Around Jaipur

There are many places to visit and sightsee in Jaipur. You can go shop for precious stones and knick-knacks in the city, or take a special safari to Amber Fort, or head for the hills on a jeep. Camel safaris for a three-kilometre ride to a maharaja's tiger-hunting ground are also available.

Location
Amla Fort is an architectural delight to behold, with bold sweeping arches and long open-terraces. It is a perfect getaway, close to major towns like Indore and the temple town of Ujjain.

Access
Airport: Indore – 120 km | **Railway Station:** Ujjain – 52 km | **International Airport:** New Delhi – 960 km
Driving Distance: From Bhopal – 163 km

amla fort
i d y l l i c   c h a r m s

Amla, Madhya Pradesh

Email: fortamla@gmail.com

DYNASTY: Amla Riyasat
STYLE: Rajput • CATEGORY: Budget

Even though the Amla Fort is located in central India, its architecture is similar to the forts of Mewar in Rajasthan. That's because the founders of Amla Riyasat who built the fort are direct descendents of Bappa Rawal of Udaipur, the brave Rajput warrior who was also the ancestor of Maharana Pratap.

Charming Contrast

The present owner, former Maharaja Rajendra Singh who inherited the title in 1948, has opened a section of the Amla Fort for guests. The fort is an architectural delight with bold sweeping arches and long open terraces.

Located on the outer western side of Amla village, the fort has a panoramic view of the fields. On the eastern and southern sides, the fort is flanked by the village and has a clear view of the village square and its activities. The stillness of life and its simplicity provides quite a contrast to the hurly burly and stress of urban life.

Around Amla

Amla can serve as a good base to visit Ujjain, the ancient temple town and centre of astronomy. The ancient temples of Koteshwar are also nearby, as is Barnagar, a centre of handicrafts and silverware. Barnagar also has a 400-year-old Jain temple.

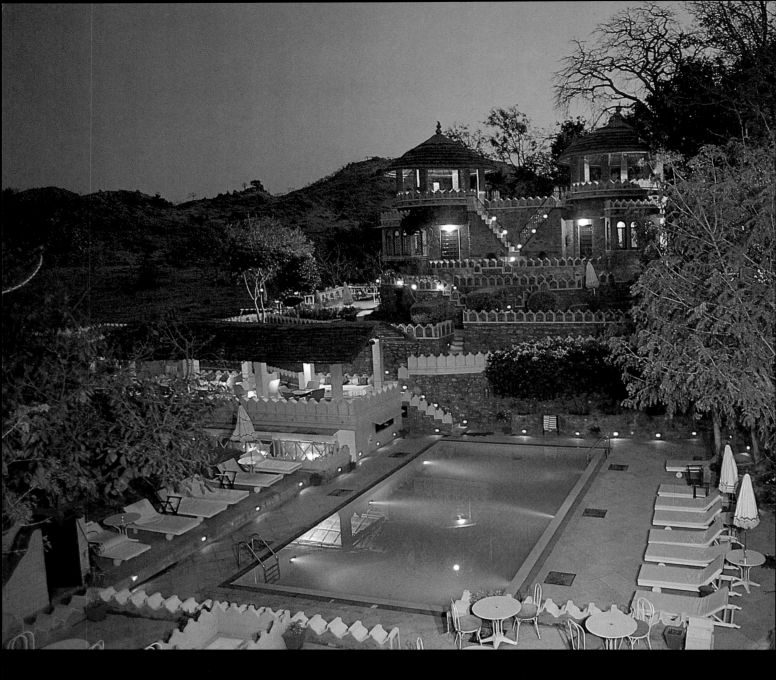

Location
The structure of the Aodhi Hotel has been designed to match the landscape of the terrain. Seemingly carved into the hillside and reminiscent of a hunting lodge, the hotel is a short walking distance from the Kumbhalgarh Fort and a few hours drive from Udaipur.

Access
Airport: Udaipur – 110 km ┃ **Railway Station:** Udaipur – 80 km ┃ **International Airport:** Delhi – 560 km
Driving Distance: From Jaipur – 300 km

the aodhi hotel
tranquil oasis

Kumbhalgarh, Rajasthan

Tel.: 02954-242341 to 47 • Email: crs@hrhhotels.com

DYNASTY: Sisodia • BUILT: Mid 15th-century
RENOVATION: 1992 • CATEGORY: Budget

The wall of the Kumbhalgarh Fort comes into view long before one reaches this 15th -century town. The 36-km long unbroken wall, often compared with the Great Wall of China, highlights the harsh beauty of the region. The credit for building this imposing fort, set amid massive ramparts and surrounded by hundreds of temples, goes to one of Mewar's legendary heroes, Rana Kumbha, who built it in 1458 upon the ruins of an existing ancient

Royal Retreat

Today, the Aodhi Hotel has made it possible for visitors to step back into time and get a glimpse of the medieval world of the Rajputs. This royal retreat has been designed to match the landscape of the terrain. Seemingly carved into the hillside, reminiscent of a hunting lodge, the hotel is a short walking distance from the Kumbhalgarh Fort.

The resort abounds in natural beauty and captures the romance and ambience of a sanctuary. It is an oasis of tranquility in a remarkable setting; the stillness and the quietness of the surroundings are only broken by the chirping birds and the call of the peacocks.

Hilltop Views

The suites and rooms at the Aodhi are elegantly appointed and most of them have private balconies overlooking the large swimming pool, green lawns, flowering trees and shrubs. The characteristic stony walls of the resort give it a rugged feel. At over 3,000 feet above the sea level, the Aodhi Hotel offers alfresco dining and a hilltop swimming pool. Jeep safaris into the nearby wildlife sanctuary, with a lavish spread for a sit-down dinner, are often arranged on special request.

Kumbhalgarh Fort

Kumbhalgarh stands on the site of an ancient citadel dating back to the 2nd century AD, which can be traced to a Jain descendant of India's Mauryan emperors. It defined the boundaries between the states of Mewar and Marwar. In its entire history, Kumbhalgarh Fort was conquered just once. It took the combined armies of Emperor Akbar, Raja Man Singh of Amber, Raja Udai Singh of Amber and Raja Udai Singh of Marwar to breach its defence. It is now preserved by the Archaeological Survey of India.

Inside the periphery wall are over 360 temples, many of them dedicated to Jain tirthankaras. The Shiva temple, which has a huge lingam, is where the king prayed.

Around Aodhi

The Kumbhalgarh Wildlife Sanctuary, the only panther reserve in India, is very close to the hotel and, if lucky, one can spot a panther or a sloth bear here. Aodhi is also a convenient base from where the ancient temple towns of Ranakpur, Nathdwara and Nagda can be explored.

Guests can visit Haldighati, where the legendary battle between Rana Pratap and the massive forces of Akbar, the Mughal emperor, was fought in 1576.

Location
A fine example of Rajput architecture in red sandstone, the Bal Samand Lake Palace, just a few kilometres north of Jodhpur, is a great place to unwind for a few days.

Access
Airport: Jodhpur – 12 km | **Railway Station:** Jodhpur – 10 km | **International Airport:** New Delhi – 528 km
Driving Distance: From Jaipur – 331 km

bal samand lake palace
splendour by the lake

Jodhpur, Rajasthan

Tel.: 0291-2572321/26, 257199 • Email: bslp@jodhpurheritage.com

DYNASTY: Rathore • BUILT: 17th century
RENOVATION: 1936 & 1996 • STYLE: Rajput
CATEGORY: Luxury

What does a maharaja do if he is bored with his palatial surroundings and wants a change of scene? He makes himself another palace, preferably not too far away from his present abode, throws in an artificial lake, builds a set of rooms on its banks, surrounds it with acres of lush gardens, develops a bird sanctuary to keep him occupied and calls it his retreat.

Lakeside Pavilion

This is exactly what Maharaja Sur Singh did in the 1600s by building a pavilion facing the Bal Samand Lake, Rajasthan's oldest artificial reservoir created in 1159 by Alak Rao Parihar. The pavilion was later converted into a summer palace by Maharaja Jaswant Singh, then renovated by Maharaja Umaid Singh in 1936 and then again by Maharaja Gaj Singh II in 1996, who restored it and added a spa to make it a complete modern-day retreat.

Outdoor Attractions

The Ayoma and Ayurvedic health spa attached to the hotel, offers several kinds of spa therapies. The palace has a multi-cuisine restaurant and a coffee shop which serve spa cusine. Here you can take a horse carriage and go buggy riding to the villages nearby. For the more energetic there is croquet, obstacle golf and a jogging trail at the hotel, or equestrian adventures, nature walks and boating. There is also a swimming pool for a cool dip at any time of the day.

Around Jodhpur

Guests can visit Mandore, the capital of Marwar before Jodhpur, to see the beautiful *chattris* (cenotaphs) of Rathore rulers like Maharajadhiraj Ajit Singh and Maharajadhiraj Jaswant Singh. The 'Hall of Heroes' in Mandore has fifteen figures carved out of a rock wall and the 'Shrine of 330 million Gods' is painted with figures of deities and spirits.

Sociologists and environmentalists enjoy visiting the Bishnoi villages, located along and off the Pali Road, south-east of Jodhpur. The villagers follow the teachings of the late-15th-century Guru Jambhoji, who outlined twenty-nine principles of nature conservation, and hold all animal life as sacred: no wonder the otherwise endangered blackbuck thrives here. At Guda Bishnoi, along the small artificial lake, migratory birds and gazelles (chinkaras) can be spotted.

Salawas is a famous centre for weaving of durries (cotton carpets). These durries are known for their intricate designs and bright colour schemes. One can also pick up hand-woven, block-printed fabric called *fetia*. Jodhpur, just a few minutes drive from Bal Samand, is a centre of handicrafts. Clay figurines of camels and elephants, marble curios with inlay work and chunky Rajasthani silver jewellery are available here.

The festival of Nag Panchami is celebrated in the honour of Naga Raja or cobra, the Serpent King. A fair is held in Jodhpur on Bhadtapada Budi Panchami (August-September) of every year. Snake charmers gather and the women worship their cobras; huge, colourful effigies of mythical serpents are displayed.

The festival of Gangaur, dedicated to the goddess Parvati, is held for a period of fifteen days following Holi. Married women invoke her blessings for material happiness, while unmarried girls pray to her for ideal husbands. The procession of the wooden image of Gauri (Parvati) is taken through the streets of Jodhpur.

Location
Deep in the Thar desert, in the city of Bikaner where richly decorated houses rise high above bustling streets, stands the famed haveli of Bhanwar Niwas.

Access
Airport: Jodhpur – 243 km | **Railway Station:** Bikaner – 1 km | **International Airport:** New Delhi – 396 km
Driving Distance: From Jaipur – 321 km

bhanwar niwas palace
jewel in the sand

Bikaner, Rajasthan

Email: bhanwarniwas@rediffmail.com

DYNASTY: Rampuria Family • BUILT: 1927
STYLE: Mix of Indian and European Styles
CATEGORY: Budget

Bikaner is famous for two things: the spicy Bikaneri Bhujiya and its exquisite art. Both owe their popularity to Bikaner's geographical location deep in the desert, where it was protected from marauders by colossal sand dunes. Bikaner's harsh, inhospitable character and its remoteness not only attracted the wealth of the outside world, but it also helped preserve its heritage much better as compared to more accessible regions.

Mercantile Riches

The Jain and Hindu bankers and merchants who, though they conducted business throughout India, settled in Bikaner with their families, collected vast amounts of treasures and built elegant homes, temples and monasteries.

The rulers of Bikaner too realized their worth and did not needlessly scare them away by excessive taxation. Thus the cultural life of Bikaner, its court and its mercantile upper class, flourished through the centuries largely owing to the treasures flowing in from other parts of India. Besides, the rulers and rich merchants of Bikaner were not only collectors of art but also offered shelter to upcoming artists from central Rajputana, Gujarat, the Mughal court at Delhi, Lahore and even from the Deccan. Thus Bikaner became a centre of later-Indian art and even developed a local variety of Rajput art.

While the maharajas built grand forts and ostentatious palaces, the merchants built mansions, albeit in slightly scaled-down versions. One such family, which had made Bikaner its home hundreds of years ago, was that of the Rampurias. In this town of red sandstone stands their tribute to Bikaner—Bhanwar Niwas.

It was the late Seth Bhanwarlalji Rampuria, heir to a textile and real estate fortune, who commissioned this mansion in 1927. He passed away in 1947 and the family shifted to Calcutta leaving the haveli empty for decades. Fifteen years ago, Sunil Rampuria, a descendant of Seth Bhanwarlalji Rampuria returned to Bikaner and converted Bhanwar Niwas into a heritage hotel. Today it stands out among the famed havelis in the city.

Marwari Victoriana

As you enter Bhanwar Niwas, you can be fooled into believing that you are entering a Victorian household. A little further inside and you can spot the Indian influences. The architecture of the haveli and its interiors is a fascinating blend of Indian and European styles. The furniture is period but there is intricate gold-leaf work on the walls done by the *usta* artists from Bikaner. Then, there are crystal chandeliers from Belgium

and antique bric-a-brac from France and England, which find the pride of place.

On the ground floor are the magnificent public rooms, including the blue drawing room and the little drawing room. The twenty-seven guestrooms, each different from the other, offer its occupants a peek into the ostentatious world of Rajputana. These rooms are a compliment and testimony to the skill and meticulous craftsmanship of the artists and craftsmen of Bikaner. The Rampurias have not only revived the art of gold leaf painting but also, for the last several years, provided employment to four *usta* artists whose job is to touch up the gold-leaf work on the walls whenever required. Being staunch vegetarians, the Rampuriyas serve the most delectable vegetarian Marwari cuisine as well as a couple of dishes done in European style.

Bikaner and Around

Motorable roads lead to the lake at Gajner, the temples of Deshnoke, Sheobari and Nagnechiji and the royal mausolea at the Devikund tank. Visitors can sample the delicious Bikaneri Bhujiya, made out of the versatile chickpea flour and available, literally by the mound, at every corner in Bikaner.

Location
The Bungalow on the Beach at Tranquebar, a sleepy fishing village in Tamil Nadu, is a perfect stopover on the way from Chennai (formerly Madras) or Pondicherry, en route to Tanjore or Karaikudi. Situated in a former Danish settlement, this small town has many historic buildings and a pristine beach.

Access
Airport: Chennai – 280 km | **Railhead:** Chidambaram – 50 km | **International Airport:** Chennai – 280 km
Driving Distance: From Chennai – 280 km

On March 1616, King Christian IV, monarch of the dual kingdom of Denmark - Norway, allowed his subjects to establish an East India Company, giving it a twelve-year monopoly on trade between Denmark and Asia. At the same time the king certified the charter of the Company. It was copied from that of the successful Dutch East India Company.

the bungalow on the beach
languid seaviews

Tranquebar, Tamil Nadu

Tel.: 04364-288065, 289034, 289035 • Email: bungalowonthebeach@neemranahotels.com

DYNASTY: Built by the Danish • BUILT: 17th century • RENOVATION: 2002
ARCHITECT (RENOVATION): Ajit Koujalgi and Francis Wacziarg
STYLE: Colonial • CATEGORY: Mid Price

The Danish East India Company focused on trade with India and had its base in Tranquebar. It lost importance quickly and was dissolved in 1729. In 1732, it was refounded as Asiatische Compagnie. During its heyday, the Danish and Swedish East India Company together imported more tea than the British East India Company—and smuggled almost all of it into Britain, where it could be sold at a huge profit.

Denmark's Outpost

Tranquebar, known originally as Tarangambadi—the place of the singing waves—owes its name and identity to the Danes who made it one of their major trading posts in the early 17th century and had a settlement there till 1845.

Almost 400 years ago, Ove Gedde, a Danish admiral, at the behest of the king of Denmark, landed on the southern coast of India. To say that he was greeted with open arms would be putting it mildly. The Nayak ruler of Tanjore was so pleased to have a visitor from a foreign land, that he quickly granted him some territory in his kingdom. Ove Gedde and his team quickly got to work and established Dansborg, the fort of Tarangambadi or Tranquebar, to begin exporting pepper to Denmark.

Today, as you drive into Tranquebar, you drive through a beautiful gate on the majestic King Street, past Lutheran churches and grand bungalows of the Danish governors and the British collector's residence. Tranquebar also became famous for printing the first Tamil Bible, again thanks to the efforts of a Danish missionary, Bartholomaeus Ziegenbalg, who arrived in 1706 and built the New Jerusalem Church just over a decade later.

But the most imposing structure is the 400-year-old Fort Dansborg, enclosed within stone walls, with cannons facing the sea. Over the years, Dansborg became one of Denmark's biggest forts, second only to Kronborg back home. By 1755, rough seas had destroyed much of the fort and it remained in a dilapidated state till 2002, when a group of Danish volunteers started the process of restoration and the Indian government followed suit. To begin with, an archaeological museum was set up within the fort's premises to showcase marine exhibits and other memorabilia, but now a part of the fort has also been converted into a heritage hotel.

Grace and Simplicity

The elegant Bungalow on the Beach is a refurbished colonial bungalow, set between the recently restored 17th-century fort and an even older Hindu temple. A verandah wraps around the eight large rooms, each appointed with period furnishings and contemporary touches.

Around Tranquebar

Tranquebar is 15 km south of the ancient Chola port of Pumpuhar, and 15 km north of the former French *comptoir* of Karikal. Here you can relive marine history and visit the temples of Kumbakonam and Tanjore.

Location

Towering high above the small town of Mandawa is Castle Mandawa: a rugged, amber-coloured fort surrounded by desert in the heart of Rajasthan. This is an ideal base from which to explore the Shekhawati region, where every home is adorned with murals and frescoes that lend colour and variety to the uniformly arid landscape.

Access

Airport: Jaipur –168 km | **Railway Station:** Mukandgarh –14 km | **International Airport:** New Delhi – 240 km

Driving Distance: From Jaipur – 168 km

hotel castle mandawa

rugged grandeur

Mandawa, Rajasthan

Tel.: 01592-223124/223432/223433 • Email: castle@datainfosys.net, reservation@castlemandawa.com

DYNASTY: Shekhawati • BUILT: 1755
STYLE: Rajput • CATEGORY: Mid Price

The best time to go to Mandawa, about 250 km southwest of Delhi, is in January when the mustard fields are in full bloom. As you drive to this medieval town, the endless carpet of yellow heads, swaying in the gentle breeze, puts you in a pleasant frame of mind even before you reach your destination.

Mandawa was the stronghold of Rao Shekhaji, who founded a dynasty here and gave the region his name. This remote principality was once a trading outpost for the ancient caravan routes that stopped here en route to China and the Middle East.

Path to Prosperity

In 1755, Thakur Nawal Singh built a fort to protect the principality of Mandawa. As the community grew and the traders and merchants became wealthier, they built palatial mansions in Mandawa and the region around it. These were decorated with colourful frescoes on every subject possible—religious to the mundane to the erotic—depicted in the unique style of the artist.

Medieval and Modern

Castle Mandawa, like many heritage hotels, is an interesting blend of the old and the new: turreted towers, winding staircases, terraces and canopied balconies blend with modern comforts in the rooms. The large and spacious rooms retain the old flavour, using period furniture and local furnishings. No two rooms are alike—there are seventy in all—and yet each of them reflects the grandeur and flavour of its past residents. In the zenana or women's quarters, the rooms have beautiful frescoes, and some even have a tinkling fountain. The rooms in the turret have walls that are said to be seven feet thick. Family portraits, antique armour, cannons—all add to the charm of this resort where tradition still runs strong. Even time is measured in the old-fashioned way here: a resident timekeeper strikes a huge brass gong at the hour.

One of the highlights of the stay at Castle Mandawa is the interaction with the gracious hosts—direct descendants of Thakur Nawal Singh—who run the heritage hotel. The verandah with comfortable, traditional wicker chairs, also accommodates the bar and is an informal place where you can catch up with other travellers. The Diwankhana, the formal drawing room, is decorated with old family portraits, wedding

and ceremonial photographs, antique bric-a-brac and an array of armour.

But the best experience of the castle is in the outdoors, whether it is on the ramparts with its bird's eye view of the faraway temples and villages or having a lavish candlelight dinner under the desert sky or sitting around a bonfire in the rear courtyard. The finale to the evening is always a performance by an ageing but zestful fire dancer who sways to the traditional beats of the drums.

Around Mandawa
The hotel also organizes camel rides in gaily painted buggies, jeep safaris, a walk through the village of Mandawa and a tour of the frescoed havelis or mansions nearby in the towns of Churi Ajit Garh, Mahensar, Nawalgarh and Fatehpur.

There are dozens of painted havelis in Mandawa, all within walking distance of the Mandawa Castle. There is the Goenka Double Haveli (built in 1890), with monumental frescoes of elephants and horses decorating its façade and Gulab Rai Ladia (1870) with elephants and camels on its façade.

Nandlal Mumrmuria (1935) has an eclectic assortment of frescoes: King George V of England, Jawaharlal Nehru on a horse and the city of Venice depicted with gondolas in its canals. Bansi Dhar Newatai (1921) has traditional frescoes along with ones that show a young boy using a phone, fancy motorcars and even the airplane built by the Wright Brothers.

Location

Excavations at Arikamedu, south of present Pondicherry town, have uncovered the remains of a Roman settlement, between second century BC and second century AD. Roman texts from the period refer to one of the trade centres along the Indian coast as Poduca or Poduke, which refers, historians affirm, to the present Pondicherry.

Access

Airport: Chennai – 160 km | **Railway Station:** Chennai – 175 km | **International Airport:** Chennai – 160 km
Driving Distance: From Chennai – 160 km

hotel de l'orient

s l i c e   o f   f r a n c e

Pondicherry

Tel.: 0413-2343067, 2343068, 2346589 • Email: l.orient@neemranahotels.com

DYNASTY: Built by the French • BUILT: 18th century • RENOVATION: 1999
ARCHITECT (RENOVATION): Ajit Koujalgi and Francis Wacziarg
STYLE: French Colonial • CATEGORY: Mid Price

The Hotel De L'Orient in Pondicherry transports you to another time—when India was the land of opportunities and exciting prospects in the West, when Orientalists painted picturesque landscapes and portraits of this land and its people, and when some marvellous architecture arose on the French coastline of Pondichéry.

In 1674 Governor François Martin started to build Pondicherry and transformed it from a small fishing village into a flourishing port-town. In 1693, the Dutch took over and fortified the town considerably. But four years later Holland and France signed a peace treaty and the French regained Pondicherry in 1699. In the 18th century the town was laid

Able governors like Lenoir (1726-1735) and Dumas (1735-1741) and an ambitious Governor Dupleix (1742-1754) expanded the Pondicherry area, and made it a large and rich town. But ambition clashed with the English interests in India and the local kingdoms, and a period of skirmishes and political intrigues began.

Lasting Legacy

The French first landed on the Coromandel coast centuries ago but Pondicherry still retains its distinctly different character and is unlike the rest of India. Walk down the high-walled streets of the old quarter and it feels so quintessentially French that you think you are in France or along the Mediterranean coast. The houses, some of which date back to the 18th century, look and feel different; the streets are laid out in a clean straight grid, the colours cream, yellow, pink and grey dominating; bougainvillea bursts over gates and compound walls of courtyards. Still, Pondicherry is not really on the tourist map, except for French tourists, though that is changing now.

Spare Elegance

For years this 18th-century mansion was used by the French Department of Education as its office, but it subsequently fell into disuse and ultimately all that was left of it were the overgrown gardens and the shell of a once handsome building. Now, it has been restored into a hotel that exudes nostalgic glamour. The building is as much an example of intelligent conservation as it is an evocation of the past, using a minimum of carefully selected furniture and art, while providing comforts unknown in the 18th century. The walls remain traditional lime-stucco plaster, while the roof has been painstakingly repaired with fresh red-terracotta tiles and the floors have been replaced with natural stone or terracotta

tiles. Each bedroom is elegantly furnished—with antiques, four-poster beds with coloured glass panels, wicker chairs and massive chest of drawers—and retains its individual character.

There is a chic little restaurant located in an internal tree-shaded courtyard that serves excellent Creole cuisine while old-fashioned punkahs stir the air and enhance the old-world charm of the place.

Pondicherry and Around

The L'Orient makes a perfect base to explore the destinations around it: Auroville, the imposing Gingee Fort, the holy temple towns of Kanchipuram, Tiruvannamalai and Chidambaram, the

heritage sculptures and magnificent rock temples of Mamallapuram, and the cool and lush hill stations of Yercaud and Kodaikanal.

The town is planned on a grid from its inception. It was divided into a French section and a Tamil section. In French Town the roads are flanked by colonial style buildings with long compound walls and stately gates. The facades have tall windows and are coloured cream, yellow and pink. In Tamil Town, the streets are lined by verandahs and extended porches where residents would congregate. Green, blue and brown dominate here while the facades project horizontal and low features.

Location
Devigarh is undeniably among the most beautiful hotels in India, a pleasant half-hour drive from Udaipur through hills and verdant forests.

Access
Airport: Udaipur – 28 km | **Railway Station:** Udaipur – 28 km | **International Airport:** New Delhi – 664 km
Driving Distance: From Jaipur – 405 km

devigarh palace

romance in stone

Udaipur, Rajasthan

Email: devigarh@deviresorts.in

DYNASTY: Raghudev Singh II • BUILT: 1760s • RENOVATION: 1990-1996
ARCHITECT (RENOVATION): Gautam Bhatia and Navin Gupta
STYLE: Rajput • CATEGORY: Luxury

Devigarh was built sometime in the 1760s by the descendants of Sajja Singh, who had been awarded the principality of Delwara by Maharana Pratap in recognition of his bravery and loyalty. Today, it quite literally straddles two worlds: though its façade remains traditional, the interiors are ultra modern and its ambience is an eclectic mix of skillfully crafted designs, old

Brave Past, Elegant Present

The original palace had been reduced to a series of small, dark interconnected chambers, infested with bats and birds when the present owners acquired it in 1990. The entire edifice was falling apart and required extensive restoration and rehabilitation work for which conservation organizations were called in.

Today, Devigarh is a distinctive, all-suite boutique hotel, evocative of a confident, modern India. The contemporary design showcased within this spectacular heritage property, with its emphasis on detail and use of local marble and semi-precious stones, goes with the new image of India.

Tradition and Change

Seen from the outside, Devigarh stands tall and impressive, pale yellow sections rising to collectively form an imposing

it is marble floors or the upholstery—against which the rich colours of Rajasthan by way of cushions or inlay work provide a vivid contrast. In all instances, the emphasis is on simplicity, understatement and serenity. The windows have views of the lush green fields and the surrounding mountains and the beauty of the locale is enough to put one in a calm, tranquil state of mind.

Devigarh, like most traditional Indian homes, revolves around courtyards—five in all—with shade trees, water bodies and quiet nooks and corners. Each courtyard blends classical and modern designs: the Kamal (Lotus) court for instance is an interpretation of the traditional lotus motif in a black-marble water maze.

The Durbar Hall, a chamber where performances and recitals used to take place in the past, is decorated in tones of gold, while the conference room is done in tones of silver, with walls in mirror work, and the billiards room is designed with

inlays of mother of pearl, malachite, lapis lazuli and other stones—have been used with great effect, lending an aura of luxury and quiet elegance to the rooms in Devigarh.

Camp Out in Style

For the adventurous traveller looking to be closer to nature, Devigarh provides six tents at the foot of the palace during the winters and spring. These recreate the tents that were traditionally used by the maharajas who were known for their constant forays into the wilderness—either to wage war or on hunting expeditions. Setting up of portable tents became one of the most important rituals, giving order and stability to their nomadic lifestyle. In order to match comfort levels with modern-day lifestyles, the tents at Devigarh are provided with electricity, heaters and fans, telephone connection and an attached marble bathroom with running water.

By climbing a few steps, guests can participate in all that

Devigarh has to offer or alternatively enjoy the simple pleasures from the sit-out of the tent—such as soaking in the sunshine, listening to the chirping birds while gazing out on to the lush lawns laid out like a mughal garden.

In Udaipur

Udaipur, the city of lakes, is often called the Venice of the East. With its marble palaces, beautifully laid out gardens and the lakes, Udaipur is like a mirage in the desert.

The founder of Udaipur, Maharana Udai Singh, had to face repeated attacks by the Mughal armies in Chittorgarh, his old capital. Legend has it that, on the advice of a holy man, Udai Singh shifted his capital to the banks of Lake Pichola—and the city was named Udaipur after him.

Overlooking the lake Pichola is the imposing City Palace, resplendent in marble and granite. The largest palace in Rajasthan, it is known for the exquisite workmanship to be found within its walls.

Around Udaipur

Several places of interest around Udaipur, including the majestic Chittorgarh, the mountain fortress of Kumbhalgarh, beautiful Jain temples of Ranakpur, Eklingji and Nathdwara and the cool retreat of Mount Abu, make the visit to the city of lakes a memorable one.

fateh bagh palace
in the lap of the aravalis

Ranakpur, Rajasthan

Email: crs@hrhhotels.com

DYNASTY: Rathore • BUILT: 1802
RENOVATION: 2002 • STYLE: Rajput • CATEGORY: Mid Price

Location
Fateh Bagh Palace was transplanted stone by stone from its original location and shifted to the temple town of Ranakpur at the foothills of the Aravalis.

Access
Airport: Udaipur – 60 km | **Railway Station:** Udaipur – 60 km | **International Airport:** New Delhi – 670 km
Driving Distance: From Jaipur – 350 km

Defying Time

The Fateh Bagh Palace comes as a bit of a surprise—no signs of a crumbling edifice here; in fact, it looks almost new and even has jacuzzis in its suites. The secret is revealed soon enough: it is actually 'Ravla Kosilav', a 200-year-old palace which was dismantled from its original site some 50 km away and recreated in its present location stone by stone (over 65,000 of them) in the same design.

Ambient Serenity

The buildings and landscaped gardens have been created on principles dictated by Vaastu Shastra, the ancient science of architecture and interior design, and make for a serene ambience. The rooms and suites of the palace have been done up based on different themes, ranging from the Vedic to folk to romantic. The honeymoon suite depicts Rajasthani love stories and comes complete with a traditional swing-bed called Hinglat.

Then there is the cuisine at Fateh Bagh where on offer is 'spiritual food' — 'meant more for the soul than the body'

— and 'Kaam Bhog' or food for love. Moonlight dinners amidst fountains and landscaped gardens or romantic lakeside picnics can be arranged for the guests.

The palace also houses an excellent library where one can pick up books on Indian philosophy, history, religion and spirituality and there are many sunlit terraces where one can read or spend time in solitude. Then there are yoga, reiki and meditation classes with trained experts.

In Ranakpur

Ranakpur is known for the marble Jain temples, exemplifying the blend of Hindu and Jain architecture, with the most intricate and delicate stonework. The Ranakpur Jain temples were built during the reign of the liberal and gifted monarch Rana Kumbha in the 15th century. An enormous basement covers an area of 48,000 square feet. There are 1,444 intricately carved columns in the temple and no two are alike. The artistically carved nymphs playing the flute in various dance postures at a height of 45 feet make for an engrossing sight.

Location
The magnificent Durbar Hall, the exclusive Gallery Restaurant and the dazzling Crystal Gallery complete the royal repertoire of unparalleled experiences at the Fateh Prakash Palace Hotel in Udaipur. Its serene premises and picturesque views of Lake Pichola, Jagmandir Island Palace, Lake Palace and the Sajjangarh Fort make for a memorable experience.

Access
Airport: Udaipur – 22 km | **Railway Station:** Udaipur – 2 km | **International Airport:** New Delhi – 664 km

Driving Distance: From Jaipur – 420 km

fateh prakash palace
still-water views

Udaipur, Rajasthan

Tel.: 0294-2528016/19, 2528008 • Email: crs@hrhhotels.com

DYNASTY: Mewar • BUILT: 1884-1935
STYLE: Rajput • CATEGORY: Luxury

You can feel the stately ambience envelop you as you walk along the corridors lined with large paintings of the Mewar School that flourished from the 17th through the 19th century. Built along the shores of Lake Pichola in Udaipur and named after the Mewar dynasty ruler, Maharana Fateh Singh (1884-1935), the Fateh Prakash Palace is a repository of exquisite chandeliers, rare paintings, and unique crystal and china collections. With its distinctive turrets and majestic domes, Fateh Prakash Palace has been classified as a Grand Heritage Palace by the government of India. Its royal legacy has been kept alive since the early decades of the 20th century when Maharana Fateh Singh used to be the royal occupant of this palace.

The Vintage Car Collection

For vintage car lovers, the Vintage and Classic Car Collection is a must see. The grand limousines and cars showcased in this new museum belong to the House of Mewar and are still in perfect running condition.

The magnificient Rolls Royce, 1939, Cadillac open convertibles, rare Mercedes models, a 1936 Vauxhall, a 1937 Opel and MG-TC 1946 convertible are on display. An original Burmah Shell petrol pump is also located on the premises, adding another authentic touch of nostalgia.

The Crystal Gallery

The Crystal Gallery is probably the single largest private collection of crystal in the world. Photography is strictly prohibited in this gallery housed in the Fateh Prakash Palace. Visitors are thus privy to an exclusive and exquisite crystal collection.

It was in 1877 that the Maharana Sajjan Singh ordered the crystal collection from the Birmingham based F and C Osler Company. An exquisite collection of crystal objets, dinner sets, perfume bottles, furniture and many other items are on display here. The Crystal Gallery also houses the only crystal bed in the world that you will have the privilege to see and simply marvel at.

Luxe by the Lake

Each suite at Fateh Prakash Palace Hotel is decorated with four-poster beds and period furniture, bedecked with velvet curtains and delicate silk tassels. The rooms and suites in the Dovecote wing, which stretches along the shoreline, have the most wonderful views of the Pichola Lake, the Lake Palace and the distant Aravali Hills, both at sunset and dawn. The rooms are decorated with original Mewar school paintings and antique Victorian furniture, including brass beds. Services also include ayurvedic massage and a beauty parlour. A palace band plays classical music in the evenings, while the library is a quiet place to catch up with one's thoughts or with some reading. For a romantic rendezvous one can take a solar or a motor-powered boat on the lake.

Location

Fernhills Palace is situated at Fernhill, Ooty, in the Nilgiri Hills of Tamil Nadu. Located in 50 acres of land with sprawling lawns, beautiful gardens and dense forests, the palace, a former hunting lodge of the maharajas of Mysore, affords stunning views overlooking lush green valleys and tea gardens.

Access

Airport: Coimbatore – 87 km | **Railway Station:** Mettupalayam – 47 km | **International Airport:** Bangalore – 300 km
Driving Distance: From Bangalore – 290 km

fernhills palace
queen of the nilgiris
Ootacamund, Tamil Nadu

Email: fernhillspalace@gmail.com, regencyvillas@gmail.com

DYNASTY: House of Wodeyar • BUILT: 1844
STYLE: Colonial • CATEGORY: Luxury

Fernhills Palace looks unprepossessing from the outside, just low red-stucco, but the interiors are amazing. A former hunting lodge of the Maharaja of Mysore, it is a repository of some of the best antique furniture—art deco dressing tables, almirahs, upholstered chairs and sofas.

Colonial Origins

Capt. F. Cotton built the first Fernhills bungalow, surrounded by 40 acres of beautiful gardens and forest, in 1844. It changed hands several times till mid-1860, when it was temporarily named Moonesami and served as one of Ooty's earliest country-club hotels. Then it passed on into the hands of the royal Wodeyar family and remained with the family.

Polished Teak, Lace Veils

The palace, superbly finished with Burmese teak, features a magnificent ballroom with a highly-valued ornamental papier-mâché ceiling. This has two overlooking galleries, one veiled with lace curtains for the ladies of the household and the other for the court orchestra.

This palace has exclusive suites, which comprise a large sitting room, bedroom, dressing room, sit outs and huge bathrooms. The walls are adorned with plaster of Paris medallions, painted red and white. There are carved cornices, moulded ceilings, wooden floors and small fireplaces in each room. Several small courtyards are a unique feature of the palace.

Around Ooty

One of the most interesting and memorable things about Ooty is the trip from Mettupalayam to Ooty via Coonoor on the miniature train. A seat on the left side ensures the most outstanding views of the Nilgiri Hills on the way up and a right-side spot on the way down. One unique thing about this train is the locomotive engine in the back, which pushes the train up the hill instead of pulling it up.

The Fernhills Palace is a good base to explore the Nilgiris hillside. Trekking across gradual slopes, carpeted with the famed Nilgiris grass is an experience unique to this part of the country. Gently curved glades fringed with a variety of ferns make for charming nature walks.

gajner palace

jewel in the oasis

Bikaner, Rajasthan

Tel.: 01534-275061-69 • Email: crs@hrhhotels.com

DYNASTY: Rathore • BUILT: Early 20th-century
STYLE: Rajput • CATEGORY: Mid Price

Location

Described as a 'jewel in the Thar desert', Gajner Palace is an intricately carved red sandstone structure built on the banks of Gajner Lake, a short drive from Bikaner.

Access

Airport: Jodhpur – 260 km | **Railway Station:** Bikaner – 32 km | **International Airport:** New Delhi – 460 km
Driving Distance: From Jaipur – 361 km

If you have made it to Bikaner, situated at the edge of the Thar desert, then a short distance away is Gajner, literally an oasis in the desert and a must see on the list of every visitor to Bikaner. A visit to the 6,000-acre property, with its own wildlife sanctuary and lake, is an unforgettable experience, tinged as it is with history and adventure.

Royal Antecedents

This imposing palace was frequented by royalty, both Indian and international, and by dignitaries. It was built by Sir Ganga Singh, Maharaja of Bikaner, in the early decades of the twentieth century. In his heyday the maharaja used it for lavish parties; Christmas was often celebrated with prearranged duck and Imperial sandgrouse shoots.

The jharokhas or windows of the palace facing the lake and courtyards are beautifully carved and its corridors are lined with wildlife paintings. The rooms are spacious with high ceilings, and have old-fashioned brass beds, carved fireplaces, antique wooden dressing tables, old English wallpaper and original carpets. The jharokhas afford fabulous views of the lake, a delight for wildlife enthusiasts who can spot sandgrouse, spoonbills and herons on the water, and an endless number of blackbuck antelope, chinkara gazelle, blue bull and wild boar coming to drink all day. The sanctuary dinners are a very special affair at Gajner. The lights of the Gajner Palace, twinkling through trees and the shimmering waters of the Gajner Lake provide an ethereal sight.

In and Around Gajner

Gajner is an ideal holiday retreat for those who love the outdoors. Here you can take a jeep, horse and camel safari deep in the interiors of the desert or explore the sanctuary. Trained guides make the safari an experience to remember, taking you to vantage points from where Gajner palace and its lush environs can be viewed.

Boating is another wonderful way to spend time in the Gajner Lake, least expected in a region dominated by the desert. There are rowing boats for those who like the physical activity or you can just relax in the solar powered boats and enjoy the freshness of a cool morning boat ride.

Location

Merging into the desert landscape is the golden hued Gorbandh Palace located in the heart of Jaisalmer, the last outpost in one of the remotest parts of India.

Access

Airport: Jaisalmer – 2 km | **Railway Station:** Jaisalmer – 4 km | **International Airport:** New Delhi – 793 km

Driving Distance: From Jaipur – 645 km

hotel gorbandh palace
g o l d e n   h u e s

Jaisalmer, Rajasthan

Tel.: 2992-253801, 253816, 253810 • Email: crs@hrhhotels.com

BUILT: Late 1990s • STYLE: Traditional Haveli Style
OWNERSHIP: The HRH group • CATEGORY: Mid Price

The desert inspires its very name—Gorbandh Palace. The ubiquitous camels weaving their way through the towns and villages of Rajasthan, all sport colourful Gorbandhs on their backs—a decorative harness made of cowry shells, beads, sequins, coloured threads and sometimes, even buttons. Gorbandhs, usually crafted lovingly by desert women for their husband's comfort, are the accents of colour on a bleak landscape.

Jaisalmer—this golden city of the desert is as magical today as it was 800 years ago when medieval merchants used to pass through it in caravans laden with precious silks and spices en route to Delhi or Sind

Trading Outpost

For centuries Jaisalmer thrived on trade and commerce and became a confluence of cultures and religions. Here you can visit Jain and Hindu temples, Sufi and Muslim places of worship, as well as quaint bazaars, ancient havelis, the famous Sam sand dunes and the Jaisalmer Fort, a majestic sentinel in the bleak desertscape. A photographer's delight, the setting sun turns Jaisalmer into a beautiful golden brown and is a spectacular sight to behold.

Poolside Oasis

Merging into the landscape of Jaisalmer is the Gorbandh Palace. Gorbandh is not a heritage property but built to evoke the authentic feel and ambience of one. This golden hued royal retreat has been built with yellow sandstone, just like the Jaisalmer Fort, and has been inspired by traditional Indian havelis. There is a central courtyard with a swimming pool, which is surrounded by sixty-seven well-appointed rooms and suites. The three suites with a private lounge area have the best views—that of the famous Jaisalmer Fort.

Dinner on the Dunes

While the palace offers traditional Rajasthani cuisine as well as European style food, the most memorable meal is the one on the sand dunes, just an hour's drive away from the hotel. The experience begins with the breathtaking drive to the dunes. The road cuts through the flat desert land like a long ribbon till you reach Sam village at the edge of the Desert National Park. The undulating dunes stretch out into the horizon and gaily-decorated camels transport guests to the dinner venue. The hotel arranges dinners on starlit evenings at the sand dunes accompanied by folk music and dance around a campfire.

Havelis of Jaisalmer

A haveli is an old-style Indian mansion, built around a courtyard with rooms arranged around it and can go up to a couple of levels. The more elaborate ones were built mostly by rich merchants in the north and western part of India, who made their money during the days when India was an outpost on the trading route between China and West Asia. Many havelis in Jaisalmer date back at least 300 years and have been perfectly preserved. The facades of these havelis are unsurpassed for the delicacy of their relief carvings, filigreed windows or jharokhas and lacelike screens.

You will find them dotting the whole town, but the most impressive are Patwon ki Haveli, Salim Singh ki Haveli and Nathmalji ki Haveli. Patwon ki Haveli comprises five ornate houses built by the wealthy Patwon for each of his five sons between 1800 and 1860. Though the houses are connected, only some are open to the public. One of them houses a boutique where you can pick up some fabulous objets collected from the desert tribes.

Salim Singh ki Haveli, near the entrance to the Jaisalmer Fort, has an interesting story attached to it. This 300-year-old haveli was the home of Jaisalmer's prime minister Maharaja Rawal Gaj Singh, also known as Salim Singh. He apparently was a particularly dishonest and greedy prime minister who extorted money from all and sundry, including the rulers. Legend has it that an irate king blew away the top floors of his house in a fit of pique. The haveli has superbly carved brackets in the form of peacocks and an elaborate projecting balcony on the top storey. There are stone elephants in front of the haveli; these were traditionally erected before the homes of the prime ministers.

Nathmalji ki Haveli, is on the road to Malka Pole. This late-19th-century haveli was also used as a prime minister's house and has a superb exterior. Yellow sandstone elephants guard the building and even the front door is a work of art. At first sight the haveli's two wings look identical but actually two brothers did the carvings separately. Local guides enjoy playing 'spot the difference' with visitors.

Location

The Grand Palace, Srinagar, formerly the residence of the Dogra maharajas is ringed by the majestic Himalayas and overlooks the picturesque Dal Lake. It is just minutes away from the city's key historic attractions.

Access

Airport: Srinagar – 15 km | **Railway Station:** Udhampur – 200 km | **International Airport:** New Delhi – 800 km

the grand palace
paradise on earth

Srinagar, Jammu & Kashmir

Tel.: 0194-2501001 • Email: wkhaliq@thelalit.com

DYNASTY: Dogras • BUILT: 1910
RENOVATION: 1998 • CATEGORY: Luxury

Jehangir, the emperor of Hindustan, was captivated by the beauty of Srinagar. 'If there is a paradise on earth, it is this, it is this,' he said and immediately commissioned the Shalimar gardens to be laid out for his queen. That was almost four hundred years ago.

Nestled in the beautiful Kashmir valley, Srinagar is surrounded by lofty snow-clad mountains. The soft murmur of Jhelum river, the serene Dal Lake, the beautiful gardens and the exquisite handicrafts make it a must-see destination. Today, despite years of turmoil, Kashmir has not lost its famed beauty, nor has the legendary hospitality of the Kashmiris diminished.

Three majestic snowcapped Himalayan ranges—Karakoram, Zanaskar and Pir Panjal—frame the beautiful Kashmir valley from northwest to northeast. It is said that Saint Kashyap defeated the demons ruling this valley and conquered it. Hence, it was after him that the valley was named Kashmir.

Nature has endowed the Kashmir valley with extraordinary beauty, as is evident from its picturesque landscapes, lush green forests of Chinar, Deodar and pine, beautiful rivers and waterfalls, snow covered mountains and a range of flora and fauna. It abounds in many varieties of wildlife, which includes bears, leopards and the Himalayan Chamois.

Opulent Origins

Maharaja Sir Hari Singh built the Grand Palace in Srinagar as his summer residence. Taking a cue from the opulent lifestyles of the Mughul emperors, Hari Singh denied himself nothing; he covered the palace floors with Bukhara carpets and elegant furnishings, and filled the gardens with elaborate fountains.

Built at the turn of the 20th century, the Grand Palace is the best place to stay in Srinagar. This two-storey heritage property with sprawling lawns has been carefully restored to its former glory and comes with all the modern conveniences.

Turn-of-the-century Charms

The palace has a Durbar Hall which is opened on special occasions for formal maharaja-style sit-down meals in a plush setting. There is an outdoor barbeque area for a leisurely and relaxed outdoor feast amidst stately gardens with flower-laden plants and majestic Chinar trees. The Dal Bar with its classic ambience offers sweeping views of the gardens and the Dal Lake beyond. The Drawing Room and the Billiards Lounge are ideal for the evening 'cuppa', a late-night drink, and a game of cards, chess, backgammon or billiards—all in a style reminiscent of the early-twentieth century.

Sumptuous Spread

For food lovers there is the regional cuisine served at the hotel. Kashmiri food is characterized by its vast array of dishes cooked over a long period of time in many exotic spices. Known as *wazwan*, Kashmiri cuisine is mostly meat based and has thick gravies, which use liberal quantities of yogurt, spices

and dried fruits. It is usually cooked in ghee (clarified butter) or mustard oil. Saffron, the most expensive spice in the world, is grown locally and used extensively to flavour the pilafs (rice preparation) and sweets. The popular dishes include yakhni (mutton curry), tabak maaz (lamb ribs), dum aloo (steam cooked potato curry), rogan josh, goshtaba (meatball curry) and haleem, which is made from meat and pounded wheat.

Around the Palace
A few yards from the palace is the Dal Lake where one can take a shikara—a gondola with an overhead canopy and silk curtains—to the floating gardens. Rising from the lake's crystal-clear waters like new growth in the spring, the floating gardens have to be seen to be believed, especially with the Himalayas forming the backdrop.

Leisure facilities at the hotel include an indoor heated swimming pool, a well-equipped health club and a shopping arcade, along with tennis courts and a putting green. Picturesque surroundings make it a haven for nature walks. The setting is ideal for cycling, trekking, fishing and photography. Guests also have access to two adjoining international-standard golf courses.

Kashmir is also renowned for its delicious juicy fruits like apples, cherries, plums, peaches and strawberries. Kashmiri dry fruits like walnuts, almonds, pine nuts or 'Chilgoza' and apricots are also known for their excellent quality.

Location

At the centre of the golden triangle of Delhi, Agra and Jaipur, the Hill Fort is perhaps the oldest heritage site in India which houses a hotel. Perched atop the rare, dark Hornstone Breccia rocks, it affords superb views of surrounding farmland and villages from its fortifications, which rise to almost 200 feet.

Access

Airport: New Delhi – 140 km | **Railway Station:** Alwar – 12 km | **International Airport:** New Delhi – 140 km
Driving Distance: From Delhi – 155 km

the hill fort
hilltop perch

Kesroli, Rajasthan

Tel.: 01468-289352/09414050053 • Email: sales@neemranahotels.com

DYNASTY: Yaduvanshi Rajputs • BUILT: Mid 4th-century
RENOVATION: 1995 • ARCHITECT (RENOVATION): Aman Nath and Francis Wacziarg
STYLE: Rajput • CATEGORY: Mid Price

At first, the Kesroli Fort appears to be quite nondescript but this feeling is swiftly dispelled as one walks up the cobbled ramp through the entrance, and into the central courtyard.

Glorious Origins

The origins of this seven-turreted fort can be traced back to over six centuries. It is believed to have been built by the Yaduvanshi Rajputs, descendants of Lord Krishna, who converted from Hinduism to Islam in the mid-14th century and came to be called Khanzadas. It subsequently changed hands, being conquered by the Mughals and the Jats before reverting to the Rajputs in 1775 when the princely state of Alwar was founded. It saw its golden period under the Ranawat Thakur Bhawani Singh (1882-1934), renowned for his equestrian skills. With thick walls, turrets and ramparts, which surround a charming inner garden and courtyards, the Hill Fort at Kesroli is an excellent getaway.

Idyllic Getaway

The rooms—some with private balconies and terraces—all add to the charm of this hotel. They all vary in shape and size. Each has a different theme, and is decorated with exquisite, colourful Rajasthani fabrics, colonial furniture and objets d'art. Outside, flowers cling to the fort walls and the dining area is informally spread over the lawns and the arched verandahs.

Around Kesroli

Just 155 km from Delhi, Kesroli is almost equidistant from Delhi, Agra and Jaipur. It makes for an ideal base to visit the Sariska tiger sanctuary, Kankwadi Fort, Neelkanth Temples, Pandupol, the monuments of Tijara, Siliserh lake, Jaisamand lake, Bhangarh-Ajabgarh, the hot springs in Talvriksh, Rajgarh, Machari, Viratnagar, Deeg, the bird sanctuary in Bharatpur, the Jat mud fort of Govindgarh and the ancient city of Mathura and its renowned museum.

Location

The Imperial hotel is located on Janpath, the famous shopping strip in the heart of New Delhi, India's capital city. The restored 1930s Victorian-style building is a perfect confluence of old-world charm and modern-day conveniences and just steps away from the renowned shopping and commercial district, Connaught Place. Museums, theatres, monuments, parks and cultural centres are within close proximity of the hotel.

Access

Airport: New Delhi – 18 km | **Railway Station:** New Delhi – 3 km | **International Airport:** New Delhi – 22 km

the imperial
s p l e n d o u r s   o f   t h e   r a j
New Delhi

Email: luxury@theimperialindia.com

BUILT: 1931 • ARCHITECT: D.J. Bromfield
STYLE: Neo-Classical • CATEGORY: Luxury

Spread over eight acres of sprawling gardens, the Imperial is a fine balance of a rich historical past with an awe-inspiring heritage and a chic international appeal. Driving down the capital's Janpath, one could very easily miss this elegant heritage hotel. Shielded by very tall palm trees, the Imperial Hotel's unique four-storey, low-rise, white colonial façade stands in quiet grace to welcome its guests.

Insulated from the commotion of a commercial district, the location of the Imperial allows for walking trips (on a pleasant day) to Connaught Place, the bustling shopping and business district. Museums, theatres, monuments, parks and cultural centres too are within close proximity of the hotel. The Rashtrapati Bhawan (the residence of the President of India), the Parliament House, and the North and South Block—centres of the administration of the government of India—are also located close to the hotel.

The Imperial, has a wonderful art collection which includes works of great British artists who worked in India in the late 17th and early 18th century and produced etchings, wood engravings, lithographs, aquatints and mezzotints based on sketches of landscapes, architecture and topography. Among some of the prominent artists featured are Thomas and William Daniells, William Simpson, William Hodges, John Zollony, James Ferguson, J.B. Fraser, Emily Eden

Class and Comfort

Built in 1931 by Bromfield, one of Sir Edwin Lutyens's associates, and inaugurated by Lord Willingdon in 1933; it was here at the Imperial where one could clink glasses on the same table as King George V or even Mahatma Gandhi. Replete with tableware from London, Italian marble floors, Burma teak and rosewood furniture, fountains from Florence and original Daniells and Frasers on the walls, the hotel is equipped to meet all the demands of the traditional traveller or their hi-tech, hi-flying counterpart.

The rooms and suites in an elegant blend of Victorian, colonial and art deco styles have interesting views, ranging from the airy atrium to the swimming pool and the well-manicured lush-green gardens. The hotel was refurbished recently and the new Deco suites are truly stunning. The Imperial and Heritage rooms are amongst the largest rooms to be found in India and, probably, Asia, some even with an area of 650 square feet. With lights from Lalique and Porthault linen, the rooms are truly luxurious in a quiet, dignified way.

and Charles D'Oyly. The hotel has three main art galleries and a collection of life-size oil paintings of the rulers of princely states of British India. Among the collections housed here are Ferguson's 'Rock-cut Temples of India' and Dodgson's 'Views in Lucknow'. The most famous collection is undoubtedly that of the oils and aquatints of the uncle-nephew duo—Thomas and William Daniell. This includes the *Oriental Scenery*, first published in 1808.

Feast for the Senses

The hotel is a veritable art gallery. No hotel can boast of such a large and amazing art collection displayed so generously in the rooms and public areas. Each floor is dedicated to an artist and their original works. It also has non-smoking floors, a selection of heritage rooms, deco rooms and suites.

The Imperial offers a bouquet of award-winning restaurants that offer a superlative gastronomic experience. In fact they are counted as Delhi's best eating places, where locals come to see and be seen. The Sixth Sense Spa has a state-of-the-art gym with treatments ranging from traditional eastern and western techniques. The Spice Route, a speciality restaurant, gives a gastronomic account of south Asian culture right from Kerala to Burma, Thailand and further east.

The 1911 Restaurant is the hotel's signature restaurant with cuisine from the world over. The verandah of 1911, popularly known as 'The Garden Party', overlooks three acres of beautiful gardens and is a wonderful place to dine, either inside or outside. Daniell's Tavern traces a culinary journey in the footsteps of Thomas and William Daniell.

the judge's court
s n o w   v i e w s

Pragpur, Himachal Pradesh

Email: eries@vsnl.com, info@judgescourt.com

BUILT: Ancestral Cottage 1705 & Country Manor 1918
STYLE: Indo-European • CATEGORY: Budget

Location

The Judge's Court in Pragpur, Kangra Valley, stands on a 10-acre orchard, just a short walk from the village courtyard, and commands magnificent views of snowcapped mountain peaks.

The hamlet of Pragpur is situated at an elevation of 2,000 feet in the Kangra Valley in the state of Himachal Pradesh, it lies in the shadow of the Dhauladhar mountains and is said to be so located as to receive the benefits of prayers that have been offered for thousands of years at three ancient Shakti temples nearby—in Bajreswari, Jwalamukhi and Chintpurni. About 300 years old, Pragpur has held onto the essence of an earlier era and remains unchanged even today.

Access

Airport: Chandigarh – 175 km | **Railway Station:** Chandigarh -175 km | **International Airport:** New Delhi – 425 km

Manor in the Orchard

The Judge's Court in Pragpur, first became famous as *Judge Sahib Ki Kothi* or the Judge's house. The property actually houses two units: one is an ancestral cottage which is over 300 years old and the other is a country manor built in the 20th century.

The cottage has been restored using original techniques but has modern plumbing and lighting. Located near the ornamental village tank and approached by a cobbled street, it houses an apartment as well as a suite and a double bedroom.

A short walk away is the large, splendid Country Manor designed in the Indo-European tradition and built as an annexe in 1918 for Justice Sir Jai Lal. This stands in a 12-acre orchard consisting of mango, lychee, plum, persimmon and citrus trees as well as exotic trees like camphor, clove and cardamom. The ten rooms go by names such as the Dhauladhar, Kipling, Hardinge and Kangra, and are tastefully decorated.

All efforts have been made by the owners of Judge's Court to make the environment natural and wholesome. All the fruit, preserves and vegetables, and even wheat, maize and oil seeds are grown in-house. Milk is from a dairy on the premises and the water is exclusively piped from an old mountain spring.

Pragpur and Around

Pragpur offers a host of activities. The village has a quaint market where several silversmiths still ply their trade and will quickly modify trinkets to satisfy individual taste. The several weavers will weave shawls and blankets to order and tailors will fashion dresses overnight.

Easy excursions are possible, including visits to the Kangra Fort; Dharamsala and Mcleodganj, the seat of the exiled Tibetan leader, the Dalai Lama; Dada Siba, famous for Kangra paintings; and to the river Beas. The picturesque Kangra valley has several spots that offer angling for the mahaseer (river carp).

Location
Nestled in the heart of the Kumaon Hills, in the small town of Binsar, is the Kalmatia Sangam Himalayan Resort. Surrounded by oaks and Himalayan Cedars or Deodars, as they are called in India, it is set amidst nature at its best. The resort can be reached via Nainital, or via Kathgodam.

Access
Airport: New Delhi – 378 km | **Railway Station:** Kathgodam – 85 km | **International Airport:** New Delhi – 378 km

Driving Distance: From Nainital – 70 km

kalmatia sangam himalayan resort

sylvan retreat

Binsar, Uttaranchal

Tel.: 05962-251176/251101 • Email: manager@kalmatia-sangam.com

ORIGINAL OWNERSHIP: Edward Thomas Chowdhury • BUILT: 1867
STYLE: Blend of British Colonial and Kumaoni Architecture • CATEGORY: Mid Price

About fifty years after the British first 'discovered' the tiny hamlet of Almora in the Kumaon hills in 1815, a young British Captain E. S. Jackson chanced upon Binsar, roughly 7 kilometres above it. The moment he set eyes on this lovely spot, with a spectacular view of the 400-kilometre wide Himalayan mountains, he decided to build himself a house right there. Toward the end of the century, Edward Thomas Chowdhury, the district commissioner of Kumaon, bought the 16-acre estate. Today, the estate and resort are presided over by his granddaughter Geeta Reeb and her husband Dieter Reeb who are always present to welcome guests to their resort.

Sunny Vistas

Set amidst sylvan surroundings, the resort incorporates a British colonial style with Kumaoni elements. Apart from the main building which houses the lounge, library, dining hall and the kitchen, the resort consists of six bungalows. Not one cottage resembles the other and all have verandahs or terraces. They are each individually designed and furnished and named after a local bird. There is the Eagle's Nest, built on two floors, with the most astonishing view of the Himalayas; the Scarlet Minivet, on the south side, has a wonderful view of the sunset and the night lights of Almora. Windows and skylights brighten the rooms to allow an unhampered view of the snow-clad Himalayas.

Homemade Zest

With a magnificent view of Nanda Devi and the Great Himalayan Range, the resort's uniquely designed restaurant allows guests to dine in comfort whilst enjoying the impressive surroundings. The restaurant also serves as an art gallery, displaying works by local and foreign artists.

Being far from the big cities, Kalmatiya Sangam relies on ingenuity to overcome the gaps in providing guests with sumptuous fare. Pickles from locally grown flower seeds replace capers in salads and pizzas. The abundant rhododendron flowers are used as base for drinks, sauces, desserts and jellies. Homemade ice-cream is made from fresh milk and from fruits such as strawberries, apricots, peaches, plums and guavas—all procured locally, some directly off the trees.

During the monsoon season (July-August) the delectable and highly prized 'Chantarelle' mushroom is harvested from the surrounding forests and added to freshly made pasta and sauces. In spring, wild asparagus is collected—young and sweet—and added to quiches and tarts. Guests are often invited to participate in cooking courses, which begin with a herb collecting expedition in the forests and the bounty thus gathered is used in the recipes.

Around Binsar

Kumaon is situated between Garhwal to the west and Nepal to the east, offering extensive possibilities of connecting itineraries, either towards western Nepal and its national parks or on the route to holy Mount Kailash. It was once a major trade link to Tibet. No wonder that Kumaon has been a confluence where cultures have blended together, leaving behind many fascinating architectural and archeological marvels, as well as charming villages where local traditions, beliefs and folklore still survive. Almora itself is an interesting blend of British colonial and Kumaoni architecture.

Only a short drive away from Binsar is a wildlife sanctuary and the ancient temple complexes of Jageshwar and Baijnath, and prehistoric rock-art at Lakhudiar. Delightful hikes from the resort lead down to the waterfalls and on to quaint Kumaoni villages with slated roofs and carved doors and windows.

Kalmatia provides as ideal base for trekkers as Kumaon lies at the feet of some of the highest mountains in the world—Nanda Devi, Kamet, Trishul, Nanda Kot and Panch Chuli.

Yogi's Wrath

How Kalmatiya Sangam got its name, is a story that goes back even further, to the 16th century, when the Chand *rajas* ruled Kumaon from Almora. Kalmatia Sangam estate stands on what was then the armoury of the kingdom. The local folklore has it that a powerful yogi once came here asking for firewood and an arrogant war minister scoffed at him and gave him iron instead. The yogi burned the iron and the soil *(matti)* immediately turned black *(kali)*, hence *kalmatiya* or black soil. *Sangam* or a confluence or meeting place was added to the name Kalmatiya by the Reebs.

Location
Situated in the heart of the residential area in the desert town of Bikaner, Karni Bhawan Palace is close to the major tourist attractions of the city like the Junagarh Fort, Lallgarh Palace, the camel breeding farm, the temples and the bazaars.

Access
Airport: Jodhpur – 250 km | **Railway Station:** Bikaner – 5 km | **International Airport:** New Delhi – 480 km
Driving Distance: From Jaipur – 361 km

karni bhawan palace hotel
desert mansion

Bikaner, Rajasthan

Tel.: 0151-2524701-05 • Email: karnihotels@satyam.net.in, vsodawas@sify.com

DYNASTY: Rathore • BUILT: 1940s
STYLE: Art Deco • CATEGORY: Mid Price

Royal Residence

Karni Singh, Maharaja of Bikaner, commissioned this art-deco style palace, taking his cue from the buildings in vogue in the early 20th century in Europe and the US. Like his forefathers, Karni Singh was a tireless builder and made this one of his private residences, even though he had the Junagarh Fort and the beautiful Lallgarh Palace. Bikaner was among the largest and the most illustrious of the former princely states of India and its legacy has been kept alive in the grand heritage palaces and buildings maintained by the royal family.

Retreat into the Past

Though the desert dominates Bikaner, its harshness has never diminished the warmth, hospitality and creativity of its people. The palace, more a stately home than an imposing citadel, has Doric pillars, ornamental brackets, decorative winding staircases and large picture windows that let in streams of light during the day.

Staying here, guests can feel the ebb and flow of history over the last 200 years. The palace has many period paintings, old photographs and English furniture in the spacious suites, the dining hall and even the corridors, creating an old-world Raj era that was prevalent in India before Independence. The rooms at this desert retreat are very spacious and are elegantly appointed, complemented by old photographs capturing the history of the royal house of Bikaner and Mewar.

Winter is the ideal time to visit Bikaner. At Karni Palace you can unwind in the hotel's landscaped gardens and the afternoons are best spent soaking in the warmth of the desert sun accompanied by a gin and tonic, a drink reminiscent of the Raj. Traditional Rajasthani and Indian cuisine, along with a selection of continental dishes, is prepared and served by the old retainers of Karni Bhawan Palace.

In and Around Bikaner

This desert retreat is near the Junagarh Fort, which may not look as imposing as other forts in Rajasthan but it is one of the few forts in India which was never conquered. It stands protected by massive ramparts and round towers, and is known for the splendour of its interiors, stone sculptures and pavilions. The fort was built between 1587 and 1593 during the rule of Rai Singh and later rulers also added to it. The Karan Mahal, with gold leaf paintings adorning its pillars and walls, was built to commemorate a victory over the Mughal emperor Aurangzeb. The Anup Mahal is the most opulent construction, with wooden ceilings inlaid with mirrors, Italian tiles and delicate lattice works on windows and balconies. It is one of the finest Rajput monuments. Raja Rai Singh, a contemporary of Akbar's, started building the Junagarh Fort in 1587.

Nearby, are the imposing Lallgarh Palace (see page 101), the camel breeding farm, the temples and the bazaars. A short driving distance from Bikaner is the Gajner Palace (see page 64). With a lake and a wildlife sanctuary, it is a must see for all who visit Bikaner.

karni fort

aravali hideout

Bambora, Rajasthan

Email: karnihotels@satyam.net.in, vsodawas@sify.com

DYNASTY: Sisodias • BUILT: 18th century
STYLE: Rajput • CATEGORY: Mid Price

Location

About 45 kilometre southeast of Udaipur, in the sleepy little village of Bambora, is the 250-year-old Karni Fort that served as a strategic outpost of the Sisodia Rajputs. Situated amidst the rolling hills, ravines and passes of the Aravali Hills, Bambora is at the crossroads of many interesting destinations in Rajasthan.

Access

Airport: Udaipur – 50 km | **Railway Station:** Udaipur – 50 km | **International Airport:** New Delhi – 690 km

Valiant Sisodias

It is difficult to imagine that 250 years ago this sleepy little village, about an hour's drive from Udaipur, the ancient capital of the Mewar kingdom, was the site of bloody battles fought by Rajput warriors defending their country. The most famous was in 1711 when these soldiers conclusively defeated Ranzab Khan and his army. For their valour and bravery, the Maharana granted the principality of Bambora to their leader Sanwat Singh. Recently the historic fort has been restored and converted into a heritage hotel by Thakur Sunder Singh of Sodawas.

Aesthetic Restoration

Karni Fort, Bambora, has been sensitively restored to retain its ambience, while offering modern conveniences. The documentation of the entire process of conservation and restoration has been showcased in the museum within the fort. The architectural elements have been aesthetically

replicated, and the original fortifications and turrets left virtually untouched. The interiors evoke a feeling of medieval opulence which is heightened by abundant mirror-work and gilded furniture.

Around Bambora

There are many interesting places to visit nearby including Jaisamand, the largest manmade lake in the region, which was built in 1691. Guest can take horse safaris to a tribal village, visit the famous Chittorgarh Fort and the Jagat Temple, also known as the mini-Khajuraho of Rajasthan.

91

Location
Perched on the edge of the great Thar desert, in the heart of rural India, Khimsar Fort stands majestically amidst acres of lawns. Situated between Jodhpur and Bikaner, Khimsar is also within driving distance of Jaipur, Ajmer and Jaisalmer.

Access
Airport: Jodhpur – 90 km │ **Railway Station:** Jodhpur – 90 km │ **International Airport:** New Delhi – 517 km
Driving Distance: From Jaipur – 330 km

khimsar fort palace
desert outpost

Khimsar, Rajasthan

Tel.: 01585-262345/46-49 • Email: holidays@welcomeheritagehotels.com

DYNASTY: Rathore/Khimsar Thakurs • BUILT: 1523
STYLE: Rajput • CATEGORY: Mid Price

Khimsar Fort's battle-scarred walls and turrets are a reminder of Khimsar's glorious past. Though constructed in 1523 by Rao Karamsi, it was only in the mid-18th century that the royal family moved in and a new *zenana* or ladies' wing was built. It incorporated finely carved windows in stone grills to provide *purdah* or a veil for the royal ladies and the ladies in waiting. Subsequently, Thakur Onkar Singh built another regal wing for himself. The fort has now been converted into a hotel, and a section still remains the residence of the 20th direct descendant and his family.

Royal Vantage

The Khimsar Fort is reminiscent of medieval India and the romance of the days gone by. The royal retreat has luxurious rooms which offer standard modern facilities that today's travellers expect. Guests here can feast in the ramparts of the fort with a vantage view of the whole city below, or on the rooftop of the dome. The theme dinners include folk dances, puppet and magic shows.

Khimsar Fort offers a welcome break from travelling and is an ideal place to unwind for a couple of days in-between visiting Jodhpur or Bikaner. The fort is great for just sunbathing or lazing around in the sprawling gardens. You can try your hand at kite flying or table tennis, watch rare varieties of birds and star-gaze at night with a telescope on the premises.

Khimsar also offers a range of safaris—you can take your pick from the jeep, camel and horses, and visit the nearby villages or sand dunes. Bicycles as well as air-conditioned limousines are available on hire for exploring the nearby areas.

Around Khimsar

Around end-January or the beginning of February there is the annual cattle fair at Nagaur (40 kilometre away), the largest and most colourful event of its kind in the country. Or, one can visit the Jain temples at Osian village nearby and the Blackbuck reservoir.

Location

The Kumarakom Lake Resort near Kochi (Cochin) in Kerala, has been exquisitely landscaped, with numerous canals meandering in and around the traditional Kerala-style Tharavad cottages reconstructed over ten acres of picturesque greenery overlooking a stretch of the lake.

Access

Airport: Cochin – 72 km | **Railway Station:** Kottayam – 15 km | **International Airport:** Cochin – 72 km

kumarakom lake resort
backwater bliss

Kumarakom, Kerala

Tel.: 0481-2524900 • Email: reservationklr@thepaul.in

BUILT: 200 years ago or earlier
STYLE: Traditional Tharavad • CATEGORY: Luxury

In God's Own Country

Lush-green palms swaying in the wind; tranquil waters reflecting traditional houses; the ever smiling faces of people as they go about their daily chores; ducks paddling in such synchronicity that it leaves one amazed; local fishermen spreading out their nets, waiting patiently for the catch; the sun rising and setting over the serene, breathtakingly beautiful waters—no wonder Kerala is called God's own country. A narrow, fertile strip on the southwest coast of India. Kerala is sandwiched between the Arabian Sea and the

The dense tropical forests, misty peaks, extensive ridges and ravines of the ghats sheltered Kerala from mainland invaders but encouraged maritime contact with the outside world. For over 2,000 years, explorers have been coming to Kerala in search of spices, sandalwood and ivory.

Kerala is also a land of rivers and backwaters. Forty-four rivers crisscross Kerala along with their countless tributaries. Rice fields, mango and cashew trees and, of course, coconut palms dominate its landscape. India's most literate state, Kerala has become a centre for Ayurveda, offering a world-class alternative healthcare system.

After an hour and forty-five minutes of a very comfortable drive from Kochi 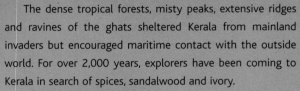 airport one arrives at Kumarakom. Until some years ago the only link to this haven was through waterways. It is often called the Venice of the East and you can arrive here by a speedboat as well.

True Taste of Tradition

The cottages at Kumarakom Lake Resort, spread over ten acres overlooking a stretch of Vembanad lake, are traditional Kerala style *illams* (homesteads) and each has a legacy that goes back at least two hundred years or more. These cottages have been transplanted from various villages in Kerala and carefully reassembled using *tachu shastra*, the ancient rules and rites of carpentry. Red stone flooring, open courtyard bathrooms with a sunken bath set in a small open-air garden, banana trees— guests are guaranteed an authentic experience.

The wooden walls are intricately carved and the roofs within the cottages are hand polished wood panels. The front doors are a work of art, banded with handcrafted brass. The furniture is antique, even the light switches and shades reflect an age when time moved at a leisurely pace. Paintings by renowned artists depict scenes from Hindu epics and have been done in the temple mural style. The traditional windows have sills where you can comfortably sit and gaze out across the lotus canals just beyond the

front yard. Or, if you prefer the outdoors, the verandah in front has the ubiquitous plantation armchairs, with extendable arms to prop your feet. All rooms overlook meandering water-bodies with floating lotus plants. At dusk, oil *deepams* (lamps) are lit all around, adding to the tranquil atmosphere.

The figure of Gajalakshmi above the portico and the *arappadi* (cellar door) in the front are enchantingly beautiful. This magnificent door, presented by King Devanarayanan, has a number of carved images like Parthasarathi on horseback and Lord Krishna frolicking with *gopikas*. Gajalakshmi in the lotus-pond is carved on the door's ivory braces.

Ethereal Cruise

Kettuvallams (traditional rice boats) glide in these backwaters, and most are equipped with modern amenities such as air-conditioning in the bedrooms and attached bathrooms. Yet they retain their traditional look with thatched roofs and lanterns. The captain, navigator and cook in tow, all dressed in their traditional *vaistis,* serve sumptuous Kerala meals, some carried on board and some rustled up as you sail to Allepey. As night falls the boat anchors in the middle of the moonlit backwaters and one can't help but wish time would stand still!

The sunset cruise is also highly recommended. As you set sail on the Kumarakom lake, musicians play the veena and mridangam. The dinner cruise is a romantic gourmet affair as the boat gently weaves its way through the backwater canals. In addition there is the popular night-fishing cruise. For an early riser, a walk through the bird sanctuary is a must. Ayurmana, the 200-year-old *nallukettu* (four-sided mansion) provides Ayurvedic care and yoga sessions.

Location

Situated on a hilltop overlooking the Chamundi Hills, just outside the city of Mysore, capital of the erstwhile Mysore State, stands the shimmering white Lalitha Mahal Palace.

Access

Airport: Bangalore – 160 km | **Railway Station:** Mysore – 9 km | **International Airport:** Bangalore – 160 km
Driving Distance: From Bangalore – 137 km

lalitha mahal palace hotel

sculpted in ivory

Mysore, Karnataka

Tel.: 0821-2526100 • Email: lmph@bsnl.in, reservations@lalithamahalpalace.in

DYNASTY: Wodeyars • BUILT: 1921 • ARCHITECT: E.W. Fritchley
STYLE: Renaissance and Indo-Saracenic • CATEGORY: Luxury

An imposing Indo-Saracenic edifice designed like a splendid Italianate palazzo, the double-columned and domed Lalitha Mahal Palace is set amidst sprawling terraced and landscaped gardens. It was built by the then Maharaja of Mysore, Krishanaraj Wadiyar Bai, to host the Viceroy of India in 1921. Designed by the English architect E.W. Fritchley, it is one of India's most opulent palace hotels, offering an opportunity to live life king-size.

The interiors of this double-storeyed palace hotel reflect the style and elegance of royal pursuits—Belgian glass dome, crystal chandeliers, ornate ceilings and polished Italian marble floors. A plethora of regal bric-a-brac accentuate the opulent tones of the lavish carvings, rich furnishings, priceless carpets, gilt-edged portraits and antique rosewood furniture. The sweep of the elegant Italian marble staircase rising to the upper floors is often used as a backdrop in lavish, big-budget Bollywood films.

The central hall is adorned with life-size portraits of the royalty, lithographs portraying Tipu Sultan's skirmishes with the British, decorative motifs on the walls and ceilings, carved wooden shutters and countless touches of regal embellishment.

Princely Lodgings

The palace has fifty-four stately suites and rooms, including the viceroy, vicerine and duplex suites which are of princely proportions. They are cool and airy, and have high ceilings with plenty of natural light, period furniture, four-poster beds, deep velvet-covered armchairs and gilt-framed Belgian mirrors. The huge, awe-inspiring bathrooms are equipped with original plumbing fixtures from Shanks of Scotland.

The old ballroom has been recreated as a gourmet restaurant and is open for breakfast, lunch and dinner. Amongst the most sought after dishes is the 'Mysore Silver' *thali* which brings together the finest array of South India's delicately spiced delights.

Outdoor activities are amply provided for with swimming pools, a tennis court, a jogging track and a golf course. Experts, headed by a team of doctors qualified in traditional ayurvedic treatment, run the massage centre, offering an elaborate massage menu to choose from.

In and Around Mysore

A short drive away are Sri Chamundeswari Temple, the Ranganathitoo Bird Sanctuary, the famous Brindavan Gardens, the great carved temple of Somnathpur, and the fort and summer palace of the legendary Tipu Sultan at Srirangapatnam. Within the city are the Maharaja's Palace, lit on select days with 500,000 bulbs, Jayachamarajendra Art Gallery, St Philomena's Cathedral done in Gothic style and the Folk Art Museum.

The main palace or the Maharaja's Palace is also known as the Amba Vilasa Palace. Designed by the British architect, Henry Irwin, it was completed in 1912. A brilliant combination of Dravidian, Indo-Saracenic, Oriental & Roman architectural styles, the three-storied stone building of fine gray granite and deep pink marble domes, is dominated by a five-storied 145-foot tower whose dome is gilded in gold.

There are twelve temples within the palace complex dating from the fourteenth to the twentieth century and displaying a wide range of architectural styles. The royal throne is made of 200 kg of pure gold!

Location
Situated in the desert town of Bikaner in northwest Rajasthan, Lallgarh Palace defies the bleak and rugged reality of the harsh Thar desert.

Access
Airport: Jodhpur – 254 km | **Railway Station:** Bikaner – 3 km | **International Airport:** Delhi – 575 km

Driving Distance: From Jaipur – 325 km

lallgarh palace

a rose red palace

Bikaner, Rajasthan

Tel.: 0151-2540201 to 07/2541509 • Email: info@lallgarhpalace.com

DYNASTY: Rathor • BUILT: 1896 • ARCHITECT: Sir Swinton Jacob
STYLE: Indo-Saracenic • CATEGORY: Mid Price

Surrounded by sand dunes and rocks, Lallgarh Palace was constructed towards the end of the 19th century by Maharaja Ganga Singh, in memory of his father, Maharaja Lal Singh.

Royal Diplomacy

Ganga Singh not only built this imposing palace, he also built Bikaner's economy and was the architect of the Ganga Canal, an ambitious irrigation project that turned the deserts of Bikaner into rich farmland. But he is best known for his spectacular grouse shoots, to which everybody from the Viceroy of India down vied to be invited. Ganga Singh very shrewdly treated these hunts as a diplomatic tool and his guests included the Prince of Wales (later King George V) and the French president, Clemenceau. Ganga Singh later led the Indian delegation to the League of Nations.

Fit for a King

The renowned architect, Sir Swinton Jacob, was commissioned to design the palace and the initial proposed cost of the project was a modest one lakh rupees (Rs 1,00,000). There were talks of reducing the costs further. But the moment Ganga Singh got personally involved in the building exercise, all cost-cutting was dismissed. Work on the palace began in 1896 and by the time Laxmi Niwas, one of the four sections, was completed in 1902, costs had already escalated ten times to ten lakh rupees (Rs 10,00,000). Cheap stucco was replaced with the finest and most intricate stone carvings and the palace was ready just in time to welcome Lord Curzon as its first important guest. The palace was further extended for Ganga Singh's son, Sadul Singh, and grandson, Karni Singh.

Royal Ambience

A complete integrated example of Indo-Saracenic architecture, Lallgarh palace is built in red sandstone. It has delicate latticework and filigree work on the balconies in the traditional Rajput style. Magnificent pillars, richly carved fire mantles, Italian colonnades and a motif of the lotus in full bloom embellish its façade, while Belgian chandeliers, cut-glass ornaments, oil paintings and antique lamps add to the charm of its interiors.

The most charming accomodation is the Bikaner State Railway saloon—with an interconnected guestroom, an attached bath and an adjoining dining room—stationed on tracks in the lawns of Lallgarh. This saloon was once part of the Maharaja's personal train.

Bikaner and Around

Of interest to visitors is the Shri Sadul Museum which covers the entire first floor of a section of the palace. It has paintings and other rare artefacts and an incredible array of photographs; and an extraordinary collection of the former maharaja's personal possessions, including an electric toothbrush.

Bikaner is famous for its old havelis (see page 32). Founded in 1486 by Bika, one of the fourteen sons of Rao Jodha, Bikaner is more popularly known as the camel country, and is renowned for the best riding camels in the world. The camel safaris, the gorgeous Junagarh Fort and the worship of thousands of holy rats at the Karni Mata Temple nearby, are some of the most interesting things to see and do in Bikaner. The camel festival at Bikaner held in January is also an event worth witnessing.

Location
Built in the 18th century as the residence of the town 'Maire' or mayor, the elegant, white structure of Le Dupleix occupies a prominent corner in the heart of the old 'Ville Blanche' (White Town) of Pondicherry.

Access
Airport: Chennai – 160 km │ **Railway Station:** Villupuram – 30 km │ **International Airport:** Chennai -160 km

le dupleix
heart of ville blanche
Pondicherry

Tel.: 0413-2226999 • Email: ledupleix@sarovarhotels.com

BUILT: By the French • DATE OF CONSTRUCTION: 19th century
RENOVATION: 2001-2004 • STYLE: French Colonial
ARCHITECT (RENOVATION): Eric Locicero, Dimitri Klein,
Niels Schönfelder • CATEGORY: Mid Price

The wooden gate to Le Dupleix is among the oldest in Pondicherry. A familiar sight in numerous photos and paintings from the colonial era, it was reconstructed with lime in collaboration with the Indian National Trust for Art and Cultural Heritage (INTACH). The gate immediately leads to an atmospheric courtyard shaded by an old mango tree. The spirit of Old France

The avant - garde and the traditional blend easily at Le Dupleix.

The Empire That Wasn't

Joseph Francois Dupleix was the governer general of the French establishments in India and the great rival of the English East India Company. He was appointed the governor general in 1742 and his ambition was to acquire for France vast territories in India. For this purpose he entered into relations with the native princes, and adopted a style of oriental splendour in his dress and surroundings. The British were worried but the danger to their settlements and power was partly averted by the bitter mutual jealousy which existed between Dupleix and the French governor of the Isle of Bourbon (today's La Réunion).

The conflicts between the French and the British in India continued till 1754 when the French government, anxious to make peace, sent a special commissioner to India with orders to supersede Dupleix. He was arrested and sent back to France where greatest of the French governors and generals in India died in obscurity and penury.

Exemplary Restoration

The restoration work on Le Dupleix took four years; traditional techniques used in the 18th century were employed by the architects and the craftsmen. Notably, the building was treated with the 'Chettinad Egg Plaster'— layer after layer of a thin coating of egg white, powdered sea shells and yogurt was applied on the walls, giving them a luminous, smooth finish.

Prime specimens of French-Indian carved woodwork has been used for the interiors—especially in the lounge ceiling

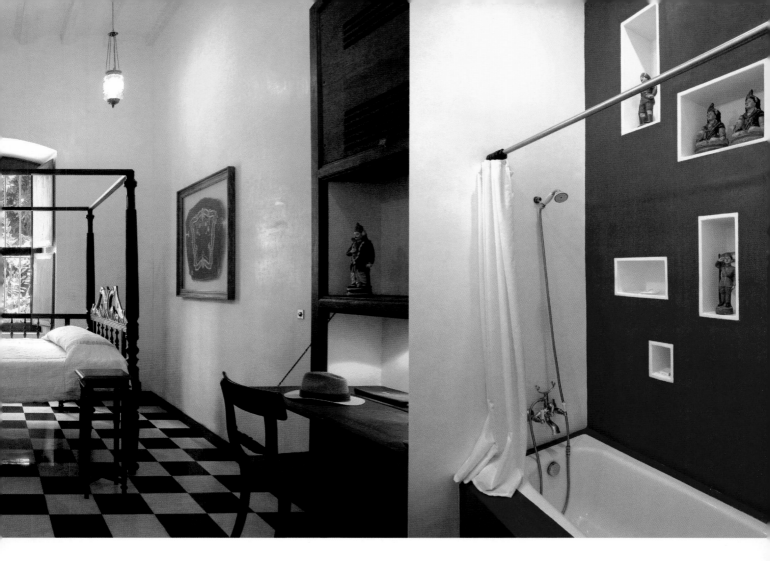

and the second-floor pillars—all of it recovered from the house of Dupleix.

The hotel has successfully achieved a balance between a traditional feel and ambience, and efficient, modern comforts and amenities. All the fourteen suites are unique in style and furnishings and, among other things, come equipped with Internet connections.

Pondicherry and Around

The old colonial part of the town flanks the seashore boulevard. Most of the government buildings are situated around the lush, green Government Park. Colonial buildings, dating back to the 18th century, lie along a grid of straight clean streets. These house French institutions, private homes and businesses, and the sprawling premises of the famous Sri Aurobindo Ashram.

The Aayi Mandapam at the centre of the Government Park is the most well-known monument. There is also the French Consulate in Pondicherry, several French cultural organizations, and even the Foyer du Soldat for war veterans of the French Army.

Pondicherry is a perfect base to explore the rich destinations around it. (see page 49) It is also a favourite shopping destination now known, among other things, for its traditional doll making, textiles and silks.

Location
Situated on the old parade ground in the centre of the heritage zone of Fort Cochin, surrounded by historical buildings and facing the St Francis Church, the Malabar House Residency offers guests the easy, relaxed splendour of a colonial villa.

Access
Airport: Cochin – 45 km | **Railway Station:** Cochin – 7 km | **International Airport:** Cochin – 45 km

malabar house residency
tropical haven
Kochi, Kerala

Tel.: 0484-2216666 • Email: info@malabarhouse.com

BUILT: pre-1755 • RENOVATION: 1995
ARCHITECT (RENOVATION): Ramesh Tharakkan
STYLE: Colonial/Portuguese • CATEGORY: Luxury

The 250-year-old Malabar House Residency stands strong and rejuvenated after recent restoration work. It is the first hotel in south India to be classified as a Heritage Classic Hotel by the government of India. Designed and run by Joerg Drechsel, who is from Germany, and his Basque wife Txuku, the Residency provides all the modern facilities in an old colonial setting.

Kochi (formerly Cochin) has a unique place in world history. Since the great flood of 1341 when Cochin became a natural harbour, it has been at the centrestage of international trade between the

The origins of the Cochin Jews are obscure although their history can be traced as far back as the 10th century when the king of Malabar granted certain rights and privileges to a Jew named Joseph Rabban. The charter, written in Tamil on two copper plates, is proudly preserved in the Paradesi synagogue to this day. The earliest known synagogues are dated to the sixteenth century. In the seventeenth century, Dutch merchants brought printed Torah scrolls and prayerbooks for them. The Cochin Jews showed their support for the Zionist movement and since 1948 the majority has emigrated to Israel.

At the Crossroads of History

In 1500 the Portuguese, led by Vasco da Gama, arrived in Cochin marking the beginning of European colonialism in the subcontinent. Subsequently the Dutch and the British dominated this sea port. A large number of trading communities settled in Cochin and, at one time, as many as fourteen different languages were spoken here. In a major step to preserve Fort Cochin's unique heritage, it has been declared a Heritage Zone.

The Malabar House's origins are inextricably linked to the history of Fort Cochin. The oldest of the available deeds documents that Jan Herman Clausing, a Dutch, bought the house in 1755 from Mathew Henrich Beyls for a sum of $756. In 1795 the British conquered Fort Cochin and the ownership passed into British hands. It changed hands a few times subsequently and the present owners acquired the Malabar House in 1995.

Seabreeze Serenade

From the hotel, at a distance, one can see the local fishermen go about their daily business with Chinese fishing nets while huge tankers and sea-liners trawl the Arabian Sea, having called at the Cochin port. Closer home, the Portuguese villas and overwhelming foliage reinforce the laid-back splendour of this coastal town.

The building is set in a garden with large trees and tropical vegetation and houses seventeen luxury rooms and suites furnished with a mix of contemporary and select antique furniture. Original artefacts, bold splashes of vivid colors and state of the art lighting create an eclectic ambience, reflecting the rich, timeless cultural heritage of the Malabar coast. Though the rooms have individually controlled central air-conditioning, they also afford natural ventilation, spacious bathrooms, and private terraces or private gardens for sit outs. The Residency also houses a swimming pool, a traditional stage for regular cultural events and a restaurant.

Today, the hotel, under Herr Drechsel, has become even more attractive. Just exploring the hotel makes for an interesting walk. The most interesting feature here is the way traditional artefacts have been contemporarized and made relevant to modern living.

The hotel offers two unique food traditions, serving a blend of European cuisines and the gourmet food of the Malabar coast. Kalari massage, part of one of the oldest schools of Ayurveda, is available as a therapy for relaxation and rejuvenation. In the evenings the stage at the Malabar House is lit with traditional oil lamps and the courtyard comes alive. Different artistes perform on select days, treating guests to cultural vignettes. A selection of local and imported wines and beers is served in the restaurant.

In and Around Cochin

All the historical sites as well as the Indo-Portuguese museum are within walking distance—the oldest existing Jewish synagogue in Mattanchery, built in 1568; the Dutch Palace with its famous frescos, built in 1555 by the Portuguese for the Raja of Cochin; the Jewtown; and the antique market, an art-shoppers' paradise.

Munnar with its tea gardens, lakes and streams up in the high ranges of the Western Ghats, the Periyar Wildlife Sanctuary in the Cardamom Hills and Kovalam, with its beautiful beaches near the southern tip of India, are all within a four-hour drive from the Malabar House.

Location
Neemrana Fort-Palace, a two-hour drive from Delhi, is an imposing bastion situated on a majestic plateau in the Aravali Ranges, representing both the strength and beauty of medieval India.

Access
Airport: New Delhi – 100 km | **Railway Station:** Rewari – 65 km | **International Airport:** New Delhi – 100 km
Driving Distance: From New Delhi – 120 km

neemrana fort-palace
stately getaway
Neemrana, Rajasthan

Email: sales@neemranahotels.com

DYNASTY: Chauhan • BUILT: 1464 • RENOVATION: 1986
ARCHITECT (RENOVATION): Aman Nath • STYLE: Rajput • CATEGORY: Luxury

A couple of hours from Delhi, and just a 100 kilometre from the international airport, Neemrana is an excellent first stop for new arrivals to India who want to take a breather. They can come to this secluded getaway that is more like a stately home than a hotel.

In 1977, Aman Nath and Francis Wacziarg discovered the ruins of the Neemrana Fort merging into the dusty Aravali Hills on a research tour while writing a book on the painted houses of Shekhawati in Rajasthan. The fort intrigued them. Along with some like-minded friends they finally purchased the property in 1986. The restorers

wanted to initiate the process of conservation and make the structure habitable. The *mistri* or master craftsmen as well as their subordinates were hired from among the local populace. Restoration in Neemrana has been an ongoing process since 1986. It is more a labour of love, aimed at preservation of heritage, than a business venture.

The process of restoration was initiated with the idea of having a peaceful retreat in a historical setting. The first phase of restoration, carried out till 1990, included the renovation of the façade in the Suraj Pol-Chand Pol area, the rampart gardens and Tulsi Chowk. While others opted out with returns on investment, Nath and Wazciarg continued. The second phase included the Holi Kund, the Aam-Khas (public area) and the Panch Mahal.

Romance Restored

The picturesque site of the fort was chosen by Raja Rajdeo and Neemrana derives its name from a brave local chieftain Nimola Meo, who, when defeated by the Chauhans, pleaded that his name be given to his lost kingdom. The fort, built in 1464 on a plateau, is an imposing bastion which sprawls vertically over several levels and covers three acres of barren Aravali hillside. Along the southern ramparts, the hanging gardens add to the rugged beauty of this fort. What was once in shambles has been beautifully restored with the aid of Indian artists and readied for the modern traveller.

Understated Elegance

Having been exquisitely restored, the finely furnished hotel rooms have canopied four-poster beds covered in colourful, delicate Jaipuri block-print fabric, matching sheer curtains and 'chik' window blinds. The furniture is a blend of traditional Indian and colonial styles. There is the old-fashioned reclining chair for the occasional nap or read. Most suites have their own balconies or terraces.

Varied Diversions

Be prepared to do a lot of walking, carry a pair of sturdy walking shoes to ascend and descend the innumerable levels of the huge, rambling building with countless wings, terraces and corridors on different levels. With superb views from the rooms, terraces, balconies and even the washrooms, it is a fascinating place to explore, whilst the glorious swimming pool with splendid vistas will tempt you not to move at all. For more R&R, there is the health spa at Yogi Niwas and the fitness centre at Chusti Mahal, where daily yoga sessions are offered. A variety of Ayurvedic treatments, including herbal baths and massages are available.

Food is a blend of French and traditional Rajasthani cuisine, served alfresco, with small charcoal stoves at the tables taking the chill out of the night during winters, while in other seasons a balmy breeze keeps the area cool.

For some stimulation and exercise, one can visit the ruined forts above the palace, or descend into the nearby 18th-century step well, which once provided the ruler and his entourage with a cool retreat in the summer.

Neemrana is extremely popular with professionals and businessmen for conferences and seminars. And often, the entire complex is booked for weddings. Art and literature festivals are also popular at this venue.

VIP Guests

Well-known writers William Dalrymple, Salman Rushdie and Vikram Seth have been guests here and performers such as the Hindustani classical vocalist Shubha Mudgal, Qawwali maestro Aslam Sabri and Sarod player Ustad Amjad Ali Khan have performed at Neemrana.

noor-us-sabah

tradition of grace

Bhopal, Madhya Pradesh

Tel.: 0755-4223333/4239996 • Email: reservations@nusp.in, contact@nusp.in

DYNASTY: Mirzai Khel Dynasty
BUILT: 1920 • RENOVATION: 1984 • CATEGORY: Mid Price

Location

Noor-Us-Sabah, the sprawling, white stately edifice perched on a hillock and spread over eighteen acres of lush manicured lawns in Bhopal exemplifies the gracious living and charming traditions of Bhopali hospitality.

Access

Airport: Bhopal – 6 km | **Railway Station:** Bhopal – 5 km | **International Airport:** New Delhi – 696 km

At one time, Bhopal, could boast of many architectural gems—impressive palaces, imposing forts and beautiful mansions. Sadly, most fell into neglect, while some were taken over by the state to house its various offices after India gained Independence.

But there is one property in Bhopal, the Noor-Us-Sabah, that has emerged as one of the very few successful attempts in the region to restore and protect its glorious heritage. The palace is now a grand heritage hotel, offering the most modern amenities while retaining its old ambience.

Light of Dawn

Noor-Us-Sabah Palace, or the light of dawn, is one of the best residential palaces in Bhopal. Built in the 1920s as the residence of Abida Sultan, the eldest daughter of Nawab Hamidullah Khan, it has all the trappings of a grand heritage property. The best feature of the property is the beautiful view of the expansive Bhopal Lake and the Vindhya ranges from every room.

A stay at the hotel, takes you back to the days when the jalopy in the drive was called a motorcar and horse carriages were the order of the day. Artefacts like the original palanquin of Shah Jehan Begum offer glimpses of the grandeur of another era. The palace is a seamless blend of old-world charm with all modern conveniences.

In and Around Bhopal

The city of Bhojpal was founded by Raja Bhoj in the 11th century, but the present city was established by an Afghan soldier, Dost Mohammed (1707-1740). His descendants built Bhopal into a beautiful city. The two lakes of Bhopal still dominate the city, constituting its nucleus. The old-city, with its marketplaces, fine old mosques and palaces still bears the aristocratic imprint of its former rulers.

The world famous Sanchi Stupa and the Vidisha caves can be seen in a half-day trip from the hotel. A visit to the old town of Bhopal with its narrow lanes and colourful markets is a must do for the guests. The other places worth seeing are the Bharat Bhawan and the crafts museum. Taj-ul-Masjid—one of the largest mosques in the country is also worth a visit.

Location

At the foothills of the majestic Himalayas is Shimla, once the summer capital of the British Raj. Situated at the quiet end of the city's Mall is the Oberoi Cecil, a splendid example of colonial architecture.

Access

Airport: Jubarhatti – 25 km | **Railway Station:** Shimla – 5 km | **International Airport:** New Delhi – 385 km

the oberoi cecil
grand heritage

Shimla, Himachal Pradesh

Email: reservations@oberoigroup.com

OWNERSHIP: The Oberoi Group • BUILT: 1884
RENOVATION: 1997 • STYLE: Colonial • CATEGORY: Luxury

The Cecil, resting at the foothills of the majestic Himalayas, is among the grandest heritage hotels of India. About 120 years old, it began its life as a small single-storied house known as the Tendril Cottage. It changed hands three times before it was finally called the Cecil Hotel.

It was first acquired by H.R. Cook and then by a well-known photographer R. Hotz. An Italian, J. Faletti, renovated the building and opened it as the Faletti Hotel.

Belle of the Ball

In the late 1930s, Mohan Singh Oberoi, India's legendary hotelier and founder of the Oberoi chain acquired the property. In fact, it was at this very hotel where he first worked and made his foray into hoteliering in 1922.

Shimla, the queen of hill stations and once the summer capital of the British Raj, has a salubrious climate which helps make it a year-round destination. It was originally a small hill village named after the goddess Shamla Devi, a manifestation of the goddess Kali. 'Discovered' by the British in 1819, it became a popular refuge from the heat of the plains of north India. In 1903, a railway line was laid connecting it to the plains and making it easily accessible. Shimla remained the official summer capital of the government of India until 1947, when India gained independence.

The Cecil was a 'hip' place to come to, both before and after Independence. Its famous balls and 'Jam Sessions' made it a haunt for the fun-loving high society that moved to Shimla during the summers. Stories are still told of Lola, the dancer, who entertained many over the years. Many a romance blossomed here and it became the favourite place for honeymooners.

After years of being the 'belle of the ball' the Cecil was shut down in 1984 and remained closed till its renovation in 1997. It was meticulously restored to a style befitting its past.

The Cecil now consists of two blocks—the main hotel and the Tudor block. The richly detailed interiors are done in warm-wood and have parquet flooring.

In and Around Shimla

The Cecil makes it possible to enjoy the Himalayas throughout the year. Situated at 7,000 feet, it commands fabulous views across the valley. The Cecil is a perfect base from which to explore the spectacular mountain scenery, the cedar forests and the ancient monasteries.

In Shimla it is possible to enjoy the unique beauty of each season. Besides the summer and winter attractions of a getaway in the mountains, the hotel is fabulous during monsoon too, when Shimla, with its gentle mists and pine-laden scent in the air, is perfect for nature lovers. The hotel is centrally heated in winters and air-conditioned during summers.

The Cecil is within walking distance of the famous Viceregal Lodge, the former summer residence of the Viceroy of India. Activities around Shimla include leisurely walks and picnics at Mashobra or Kufri. The Cecil staff has charted several interesting heritage-site walks within the city, including the Gaiety Theatre which once staged productions from London, and the colonial buildings and the church on the main promenade. A nine-hole golf course is also within easy driving distance of Shimla.

Location

The Oberoi Grand, the premier business hotel in Kolkata, the capital of West Bengal, is known for its old-world charm and quality service. The hotel is centrally located on Jawahar Lal Nehru Road, popularly known as Chowringhee, the main business and shopping district of Kolkata.

Access

Airport: Kolkata – 22 km | **Railway Station:** Howrah – 6 km, Sealdah – 3 km | **International Airport:** Kolkata – 22 km

the oberoi grand
grande dame of kolkata

Kolkata, West Bengal

Tel.: 033-22492323 • Email: reservations@oberoigroup.com

OWNERSHIP: The Oberoi Group • BUILT: 1870s
STYLE: Victorian • CATEGORY: LUXURY

The Oberoi Grand is a part of the Kolkata (formerly Calcutta) cityscape; it has witnessed and shared in all that the city has been through. It added oomph and glamour during its heyday, and sheltered soldiers returning from World War II. It was an eyewitness to famine and floods, the passing of an empire and a bloody independence. The Grand is affectionately known as the 'Grande Dame of Calcutta'.

Founded by Job Charnock, an agent of the East India Company, in 1690, Kolkata became the capital of British India in 1772, which it remained till 1912, when the British moved the capital city to Delhi. In its heyday Calcutta (as it was called till 2001) was known as the Second City of the British Empire.

Colonial Origins

It started out as a mansion of one Col Grand, who won plot No.13, Chowringhee, in a lottery and built a house on it patterned on a county seat. In the 1870s, a Mrs Monk ran it as a boarding house for travellers, which became so popular that it soon extended from No. 13 right up to No.17, Chowringhee.

In 1943, the legendary hotelier of India, Rai Bahadur Mohan Singh Oberoi, bought the hotel. It was used to accommodate 2,000 Allied soldiers during World War II. Today it is among the leading hotels of the world. Of course, the hotel looks nothing like Col Grand's mansion but the first owner's name endures to this day.

Heritage in Style

The Oberoi Grand's neo-classical façade and grand pillared entrance mark a successful fusion of the classical and traditional Indian style, and reflect the city's colonial heritage.

Located in the heart of Calcutta's commercial district and shopping centre, the hotel makes an impressive, luxurious and convenient base for a business trip. Cool green marble floors, Corinthian columns, balustrades, classical pediments and palms, all lend it an air of turn-of-the-century colonial grandeur.

The hotel has three wings: Lindsay, Roxy and Chowringhee—named after the roads they face. All rooms and suites convey the same sense of space, elegance and gracious living, while providing every convenience that the modern traveller has come to expect. Having played host to former princes and dignitaries such as the French president Francois Mitterrand and the famous author of *The City of Joy*, Dominique Lapierre, the hotel boasts of impeccable service standards. Some rooms have city views while others face the gardens. All the rooms and suites at the Grand are elegantly chic and very comfortable.

The spa-therapy suites are the place to unwind after a hard day's business or sightseeing. Managed by the world famous Banyan Tree and staffed by trained Thai therapists, it offers guests a comprehensive range of holistic therapies and treatments, including aromatherapy and Ayurvedic, Thai, Balinese, Indian and Hawaiian massages. Golf, horse riding, squash and tennis are all also available within easy driving distance of the hotel.

In Kolkata

There are many facets to Kolkata. For one, it is a reputed centre of culture, famed for its cinema, poetry, music and art. It also offers up some wonderful memorabilia of the British Raj. But, above all, Kolkata is an intensely human city and the warmth and charm of its people is to be experienced to be believed.

Some interesting places to visit in Kolkata are Dalhousie Square (renamed Benoy-Badal-Dinesh Bagh after the three martyrs of Bengal), which was created in the heart of the imperial capital of Calcutta. The tank in the centre, fed by natural springs, is said to have supplied Job Charnock—the founder of Calcutta—with drinking water. Historical buildings such Writers' Building; Raj Bhavan, residence of the Governor; the State Legislative Assembly House and the Calcutta High Court surround the square. Netaji Subhash Road is where the offices of onetime English commercial houses—now flourishing in Indian hands—are located. Lyon's Range stock exchange, behind Clive Street, is worth a visit for a glimpse of the frenzied dealing in shares, periodically erupting onto the street.

The Gothic St. Paul's Cathedral has exquisite scriptural scenes and a communion plate presented by Queen Victoria. The candlelight service on Christmas Eve is a moving experience. The Howrah Bridge, dominating the Kolkata skyline, is a major landmark and so much a part of the city that Kolkata is inconceivable without it. Opened in 1943, replacing a pontoon bridge, it is today one of the busiest bridges in the world. And, there is the Victoria Memorial, close to the Grand. It is a magnificent structure combining the best of Western and Indian architectural styles and houses a museum of British-India memorabilia.

Location

Maidens hotel, Delhi, described as an 'old-world grand dame' has a quaint charm to it. While its location in the older part of the city allows its guests to escape the noise of the city, it is still within easy distance of Delhi's historic monuments and shopping areas.

Access

Airport: New Delhi – 24 km | **Railway Station:** New Delhi – 10 km | **International Airport:** New Delhi – 27 km

the oberoi maidens

old-world aura

Delhi

Tel.: 24363030 • Email: reservations@oberoigroup.com

OWNERSHIP: The Oberoi Group • BUILT: 1898
STYLE: COLONIAL • CATEGORY: Luxury

'Send money or can remain Maidens no more,' wired three young English ladies in the 1920s, who had overrun their budget while staying at the Maidens, Delhi's most fashionable hotel. This amusing anecdote has been well documented by historians of Delhi and by the Maidens hotel too.

Georgian Beauty

This Georgian beauty, clad in white, opened in 1898 when the plans for the city of New Delhi were still being finalized by its architect Edwin Lutyens. In fact, it is said that he stayed at the Maidens during this period.

From being the centre of activity during the Raj, the hotel is now a bit off the beaten track, but away from the noise and the crowd. Just a half-hour drive from New Delhi's Connaught Place, it serves as a charming, old-fashioned retreat, yet is within easy distance of Delhi's historic monuments and shopping areas. The hotel is immensely popular with old Raj hands looking for some nostalgia and, surprisingly, young couples looking to adopt children from the nearby orphanage.

Scrapbook of the Raj

The Maidens is a low lying colonial building which has thankfully remained the way it was, though some efforts at modernizing it have made it more comfortable for today's travellers. As a result, the long verandahs have been glazed for central air-conditioning, the restaurant has been smartened up and there is also a cozy bar; but the Doric columns, stained-glass windows, old photographs and huge spacious rooms remind one of the days when Delhi was still coming into its own as the capital of India.

Walking into the Curzon Room, the restaurant at the Maidens, is like walking into a scrapbook of the Raj. There are columned walls, white linen and old photographs which render a pictorial history of the British Raj. Lord Curzon was the Viceroy of India at the turn of the last century when the Indian princes held the Delhi Durbar in 1903—a spectacular reception for the British royal family. Curzon, whether hunting tigers or at the Delhi Durbar, features prominently in the pictures.

The rooms at the Maidens, probably the most spacious in Delhi, have high ceilings, roomy bathrooms and most have separate sitting rooms. Originally designed for the hot summer months, they are set on the inside. However, there are extensive lawns, a quaint kidney shaped swimming pool and an alfresco restaurant where one can lounge for hours. Here one can listen to birds, rest under ancient trees, sunbathe or even play tennis.

In and Around Delhi

Delhi is one of the oldest cities in the world. In keeping with its rich past, Delhi has some magnificent monuments from the ancient, medieval and the modern period—there is the Purana Quila, Qutub Minar, Tughlaquabad Fort, Ferozeshah Kotla, Lodhi's Tomb, Humayun's Tomb, the Red Fort, Safdarjang's Tomb, the Jama Masjid and Jantar Mantar, the astronomical observatory built in 1724.

The relatively newer architectural attractions include the India Gate, the Parliament House, Raj Ghat—the memorial to Mahatma Gandhi, and Lotus Temple—the Bahai's House of Worship. Old Delhi with its historic narrow *gullies*, its crowd, colour and barely controlled chaos is a perennial favourite with tourists.

Location

The Old Bungalow and the Writers' Bungalow are located in the fruit basket of the Kumaon region in the foothills of the Himalayas. These heritage homes once housed the British and Indian officers and their wives, and could be reached only on horseback and palanquins.

Access

Airport: Pantnagar – 80 km | **Railway Station:** Kathgodam – 38 km | **International Airport:** New Delhi – 325 km
Driving Distance: From Nainital – 25 km

the ramgarh bungalow
verdant tranquillity

Ramgarh, Uttaranchal

Tel.: 05942-281156, 281137 • Email: sales@neemranahotels.com
OWNERSHIP: Neemrana Hotels • RENOVATION: 1996
BUILT: The Old Bungalow - 1830 & The Writers' Bungalow -1860
ARCHITECT (RENOVATION): Aman Nath • STYLE: Colonial • CATEGORY: Mid Price

Nothing prepares you for the quiet beauty of the Kumaon hills. Once you leave noisy Kathgodam on the foothills and the relatively quieter Bhimtal behind you and wind your way further up to Ramgarh, you can feel the quality of air change with every serpentine curve you negotiate. Suddenly, there is much less traffic, just long stretches of empty road and hills towering above you. Time seems to stand still here and the silence is only broken by the occasional dog barking somewhere or villagers talking softly as they make their way back home. There are no bright lights, just scattered huts and dimly lit tiny shops along the edge of the highway. The only thing in abundance here is tranquillity and, of course, nature in all its green finery.

Famous Residents

It's no wonder that many writers and thinkers have been drawn to the beauty of Ramgarh: Sri Aurobindo and Narain Swami established ashrams here, Nobel Laureate Rabindranath Tagore wrote some of his major works including *Geetanjali* amidst these serene environs. It is believed that he even contemplated founding his famous school Shantiniketan here; celebrated Indian author Mahadevi Verma made it her home and some of India's leading industrial families own sprawling orchards in these sylvan surroundings.

Peace, Quiet and Good Cheer

Beautifully preserved, the bungalows reflect that old-world charm of the colonial era. While restoring the structure, care has been taken to retain all the unique and characteristic features of the original—bay windows, the verandah and the antique furniture, among other things. There has been no additional construction, no marble flooring, and no frills and fancies. To spend time here is a true holiday: there is no Internet or fax connection here and even mobile phones do not work.

Each suite of the Old Bungalow—the Kumaon, the Kashmir and the English—is unique, with its own character and colour themes inspired by the Kumaoni countryside. The panoramic vistas from the bungalows are truly awesome. Early risers can catch a spectacular sunrise, while tired eyes can soak in the verdant greens. Wild flowers and sprawling orchards provide a picturesque backdrop, no matter where you are. The Writer's Bungalow is situated above the Old Bungalow and is just a five-minute walk uphill. The charming suites in cheerful colours have a writing table and antique beds and provide an ideal atmosphere for those who want solitude and quiet.

Around Ramgarh

From May to September the orchards by the bungalows hang with apricots, plums, peaches, pears and apples. Jungle walks and trekking, bird watching, boating in Nainital and a visit to Mukteshwar are some of the activities that can be done with the Bungalows as your base.

The fair at Gananath (47 kilometre from Almora) on Kartik Poornima attracts thousands of pilgrims who come to worship Lord Shiva and Ganesha.

The word Kumaon is derived from the word 'Kurmanchal' meaning Land of the 'Kurm' avatar. The reference is to the tortoise incarnation of Lord Vishnu, who is the preserver in the Hindu Trinity.

In the hills of Kumaon, Lakshmi Puja—worship of Lakshmi the goddess of wealth—is performed in a unique way. Three sugarcane sticks are placed like a tripod in a large plate and a fruit like malta or orange is placed in the centre. This is covered with a red *chunni* with golden lining. This, along with silver coins, is worshipped as Lakshmi.

Location

The Palace Belvedere is set amongst the Kumaon hills in Nainital. The hotel affords a panoramic view of the famous Naini Lake, which finds mention as a place of meditation in the ancient *Skanda Puranas*, which originated as an oral tradition around 1500 BC.

Access

Airport: New Delhi – 326 km | **Railway Station:** Kathgodam – 35 km | **International Airport:** New Delhi – 326 km
Driving Distance: From Dehradun – 387 km

the palace belvedere
summer escape
Nainital, Uttaranchal

Tel.: 05942-237434/231889 • Email: belvederepalace@rediffmail.com

DYNASTY: Rajas of Awagarh • BUILT: 1897
STYLE: Colonial • CATEGORY: Mid Price

Nestling snug in one of the most popular hill resorts of India, Nainital, is the summer palace of the Rajas of Awagarh—The Palace Belvedere. Built by Raja Balwant Singh of Awagarh in 1897, the Palace Belvedere today stands for regal and gracious living. The rooms and suites offer a panoramic view of the famous Naini Lake. Now renovated and refurbished, this stately colonial mansion still retains its unique, original and highly distinctive character, and is run as a heritage hotel under the personal supervision of the current members of the royal family.

Stately Grace

The Belvedere has a façade in stone and is edged in white. Pine-scented breeze wafts through the open, colonnaded patio on the ground level located adjacent to the lounge and dining area. A large sweeping staircase from the central hallway leads to the rooms on the second level, of which seven are facing the lake. The hotel has a two-bedroom family suite that runs along the length of the frontage. The rooms are vast and spacious, almost like mini-apartments, with huge bathrooms. Though situated in close proximity to the town, the hotel is surrounded by sprawling gardens—a befitting setting for the regal estate.

In and Around Nainital

Nainital's most prominent feature is the beautiful Naini Lake surrounded by high mountains. Skirting the lake is a café-studded promenade for leisure walks and endless 'cuppas'. The boat club here offers pedal boats, sailboats and even rowboats for enthusiasts. The Club House emanates an old-fashioned flavour that comes through its creaking teak floors. A restaurant at the deck serves good Indian food and makes for a pleasant way to spend the evenings. The salubrious and invigorating climate delights the visitors in all seasons, with its kaleidoscope of colour and beauty.

Guest can drive to Land's End to view the magnificent terrace fields, trek to Naini Peak, the highest point in the area. They can go to Snow View and see the panoramic sweep of snow-clad Himalayan peaks and visit Dorothy's Seat—a memorial to an English lady.

Location

The grand Piramal Haveli is located in the Shekhawati region of Rajasthan, famous for its painted havelis belonging to wealthy Marwaris, a self-contained community of merchants. Built in the traditional style with four courtyards and large open gardens, it has charming frescoes of flying angels and gods in motorcars.

Access

Airport: Jaipur – 190 km | **Railway Station:** Jhunjhunu – 15 km | **International Airport:** New Delhi – 250 km
Driving Distance: From Jaipur – 190 km

piramal haveli

stone canvas

Bagar, Rajasthan

Tel.: 01592-221220 • Email: sales@neemranahotels.com

DYNASTY: Built by Seth Piramal Chaturbhuj Makharia
BUILT: 1892-1958 • RENOVATION: 1993
ARCHITECT (RENOVATION): Aman Nath and Francis Wacziarg
STYLE: Rajasthani-Colonial • CATEGORY: Mid Price

The region of Shekhawati, in the northwest corner of Rajasthan was founded by Rao Shekha (1433-1488) and was an independent kingdom from 1471 till 1738, when it reverted back to the Jaipur State.

Through the centuries, the towns of Shekhawati grew in importance and were vital trading posts on the route between China and West Asia. Camel led caravans loaded with goods like silks, brocades, saffron, opium, tobacco and tea would pass through the dusty region of Shekhawati, making the merchants dealing in these goods prosperous.

Riot of Colours

As these merchants grew richer, they built huge mansions for their families. Thus the villages and towns of this arid and dry region were dotted with hundreds of elaborate mansions covered with frescoes and murals in bright colours ranging from blues to yellows and greens—both inside and outside. The themes of the murals were eclectic, ranging from the royal to the religious to the erotic.

Soon after India became independent, Shekhawati lost its importance and within a few years the rich merchants abandoned their homes and moved to other cities. Their havelis lay in disuse; and many collapsed and turned into rubble. Others were vandalized and in some, shockingly, the paintings were painted over. But conservationists swung into action and rescued these painted havelis from oblivion. Today, the frescoes of Shekhawati attract tourists from all over the world and many mansions that still exist belong to influential Marwari industrialists.

Gods Behind the Wheel

The Piramal Haveli was the home of Seth Piramal Chaturbhuj Makharia (1892-1958) who made his fortune in Bombay, trading in cotton, opium, silver and other commodities. Built in the Rajasthani-Colonial style of the 1920s, the haveli has traditional courtyards enclosed by colonial pillared corridors. Frescoes of flying angels and gods in motorcars adorn its walls.

The large *baithak* (drawing room) has a striking fresco on the ceiling. These kitsch frescoes add to the charm of the haveli and reflect the British presence in Jaipur since 1803. Here, the famed vegetarian cuisine of the Marwaris is served in traditional *thalis*. Dinners on the sand dunes can also be arranged.

Though the towns of Shekhawati are trying hard to catch up with the rest of urban India, the villages seem unchanged, as if caught in a time warp.

Around Bagar

Just walking down the streets of Shekhawati is an interesting experience in itself. Its painted havelis have made this small principality famous the world over and caught the imagination of many a traveller. Many havelis are open to the public, some have an entrance fee and some may even refuse entry. While in Shekhawati one can visit the Sati temple in Jhunjhunu and the old step-well in Nawalgarh.

Location

The Rambagh is located in the heart of Jaipur. Amidst the Pink City's bustling bazaars and forts, its forty-seven acres of landscaped gardens offer a haven of tranquillity.

Access

Airport: Jaipur – 11 km | **Railway Station:** Jaipur – 5 km | **International Airport:** New Delhi – 250 km

rambagh palace
regal luxury revived

Jaipur, Rajasthan

Tel.: 0141-2211919 • Email: rambagh.jaipur@tajhotels.com

DYNASTY: Kachhwaha Rajputs • BUILT: 1835 • RENOVATION: 1957
ARCHITECT: Sir Swinton Jacob • STYLE: Rajput and Mughal
CATEGORY: Luxury

Until 1957, the Rambagh Palace was the home of the Maharaja of Jaipur and his wife, the legendary Gayatri Devi—regarded as one of the most beautiful women of the world.

The Rambagh's special status was reflected in its name, the 'Jewel of Jaipur'. The palace has played host to several royal guests, including Queen Elizabeth and Prince Philip, and numerous lavish banquets and celebrations have been held here over the years. Today the palace is open

Popularly known as the Pink City, Jaipur, was founded in 1727 by one of the greatest rulers of the Kachhawaha clan, the astronomer king Sawai Jai Singh. The growing population and the paucity of water prompted him to shift the capital of his kingdom from Amber. The pink color was used when the city—which he named after himself—was being built, so as to create a likeness of the of red sandstone favoured by the Mughals.

Pioneering Hotelier

Built in 1835 on a modest scale for the queen's favourite handmaiden, it was later refurbished as a royal guesthouse and hunting lodge. In 1931, Maharaja Mansingh enlarged the palace even further and modernized it. Nine years later, when Maharaja Mansingh married Princess Gayatri Devi, he revamped the royal suites. In December 1957 the Rambagh Palace Hotel was formally opened and the Maharaja of Jaipur became India's first active royal hotelier.

History and High Living

The Rambagh is an architectural masterpiece, blending elements of Rajput and Mughal architecture. If the colonnaded corridors with potted palms, marbled courtyards and fretted screens all speak of history and legend, it is because the Rambagh has been home to two generations of royals.

Today it is among the most popular luxury hotels in India. The rooms are beautifully furnished and offer all the modern facilities; superior rooms are tastefully decorated in Rajasthani

The maharaja and his chief architect, Vidyasagar, planned the city. Jai Singh's scientific bent of mind is reflected in the precise symmetry of the new city, which provides quite a contrast to the typical unplanned, labyrinthine north Indian city. Jaipur was laid out according to the strict principles of town planning set down in the *Shilpa Shastra* – the ancient Hindu text of architecture.

style with the colours and weaves made famous all over the world by local artisans.

Among the royal suites, visitors can choose from among the Maharaja suite with a large canopied bed, the Maharani suite with a mirrored bathroom and the Princess suite with its own fountains and private terrace garden. Carefully restored with period furniture, and with large French windows overlooking the gardens, the suites have been occupied by international dignitaries, celebrities and heads of state.

The palace gets its name ('bagh' means garden) from the beautiful gardens that surround it. The rooms overlook courtyards with fountains, open out onto airy verandahs or offer views of vast lawns dotted with mango trees.

Unwinding in Style

After a visit to the city, it is great to come back to the Rambagh. In the evenings have a drink on the verandah with its pillars and arches. Occasionally, there are peacocks strutting

145

on the lawns. And if it is raining, the mango trees and gardens turn a dark shade of green.

Indian royalty is known for their equestrian prowess and some of the glamour of royal polo matches is on display in the Polo Bar. Trophies and memorabilia adorn the walls while the bar staff serve signature cocktails inspired by this royal sport.

The indoor pool, amid the intricate fretted screens and stained-glass panels, used to be a favourite retreat of the royals. Today, the weather-controlled pool and the adjoining courtyard provide a private sanctuary where guests can unwind, read or sunbathe.

The Rajput Room is the informal all-day restaurant overlooking the front lawns. Beyond these lawns rises the fairytale castle—Moti Doongri. Originally built as a battle outpost, the 400-year-old fort was renovated to serve as the royal residence of Gayatri Devi when she came as the maharaja's new bride. With prior permission, private excursions can be arranged for guests.

Jaipur, admittedly, was first not an aesthetic triumph, but its stout walls served to protect its inhabitants from invaders, and encouraged merchants and traders to flock here. This led to the city's growth and prosperity. Jai Singh's interest in the arts and sciences fostered their development, and the royal court became a centre of intellectual and artistic endeavour.

Location
The 150-year-old Samode Palace stands in sprawling splendour on a hilltop at the end of a dusty road. An hour's drive from Jaipur, this magnificent example of Rajput-Mughal architecture, boasts some of the finest frescoes and mirror-work in Rajasthan.

Access
Airport: Jaipur – 56 km | **Railway Station:** Jaipur – 40 km | **International Airport:** New Delhi – 250 km
Driving Distance: From Jaipur – 56 km

samode palace

desert bloom

Samode, Rajasthan

Tel.: 0141-2632370 • Email: reservations@samode.com

DYNASTY: Kachhwaha • BUILT: Early 19th-century
RENOVATION: 1987 • STYLE: Rajput-Moghul • CATEGORY: Luxury

Approximately 40 kilometre northwest of Jaipur, Samode Palace nestles among the Aravali ranges and comes into view like a mirage rising above the cobbled streets and stone houses of the village of Samode.

For the first half of its existence, Samode Palace was little more than a fortified stronghold in a small principality. It was only in the early 19th century under Rawal Berisal that the castle began to take on the lavish aspects it is now known for. The expansion of Samode Palace began during his reign and continued under his descendant Rawal Sheo Singh, who was also the prime minister of the Jaipur State in the mid-19th century.

VIP Haunt

It's quite possible to bump into singer Mick Jagger, actor Jeremy Irons or the British designer and tastemaker Lulu Guinness or any of the Indian film stars at the Darbar Hall at Samode Palace. Once the sole preserve of the princes, the Samode Palace today is a luxury hotel which attracts a galaxy of celebrities from the world of stage, screen, fashion, politics and royalty. Well-heeled travellers and guests come here to experience India's rich history and majesty in true luxury.

Dazzling Detail

It was in 1987 that Samode Palace, a perfect example of Rajput-Mughal architecture, was transformed into a palace hotel. Built on a small hillock, it is planned in a progression of courtyards of increasing height, endless wings, terraces and lavish creations like the extravagantly painted Durbar Hall and the breathtaking Sheesh Mahal. Twisting staircases and painted corridors open into rooms and suites.

The interiors, inspired by traditional themes, reach their fullest expression in the intricate marble-work, woodwork and fabrics. Scattered around the building, the rooms vary in size, shape and design, but all are colourful and unique with intricate marble and mosaic floorings, high ceilings, *durries* (woven cotton rugs), antiques and beautifully carved four-poster beds which are tastefully decorated with some of Jaipur's finest block-printed fabrics and woodwork. As befits a palace, they are all stunningly designed with latticed windows, motifs painted on walls and ceilings, and have spacious living area. Most have views of the walled gardens and valley; others have balconies, views of the village, mountains or the Samode Fort. The spectacular royal suites on the top floor have private balconies and jacuzzis in the bedroom.

In and Around Samode

Guest can take day trips to the museums and bazaars in the historic cities of Jaipur and Amber. They can also spend time exploring the village of Samode on foot, cycle, camel back or horseback, or simply relax and enjoy a picnic lunch in the mango orchard or Samode Bagh (the garden resort) nearby. The more adventurous can ride the horses up the hillocks into the sand dunes. Those with energy to burn can climb the 376

steps up a mountain by the palace to the Samode Fort that once protected Samode. The climb is steep but the views across the valley make it worth the effort.

    After a day's sightseeing, one can unwind with an Ayurvedic massage or laze by the marble-mosaic pool set in a tranquil walled garden with views of the Aravali hills. The palace overlooks a 12th-century manmade lake and sprawling gardens. Though winter is the best time to visit Samode, the palace offers a cool respite in the unbearably hot summer months too. During winters the lake and surrounding wooded areas become home to different species of migratory birds such as the Imperial Sandgrouse. Endangered antelopes like blackbucks, nilgais, chinkaras and other animals like the wild boar roam freely in this area which is now a preserved

Location

Shikarbadi, just 4 kilometre from Udaipur, was formerly the hunting lodge of the royal Mewar family. Set against the Aravali hills, amidst breathtaking countryside which includes a lake, it continues to preserve the rugged ambience of a sanctuary with chalet style accommodation.

Access

Airport: Udaipur – 30 km | **Railway Station:** Udaipur – 4 km | **International Airport:** New Delhi – 664 km

Driving Distance: From Jaipur – 420 km

shikarbadi hotel
idyllic sanctuary

Udaipur, Rajasthan

Tel.: 0294-2583200 to 04 • Email: crs@hrhhotels.com

DYNASTY: Mewar • BUILT: 1930
RENOVATION: 1975 • CATEGORY: Mid Price

Shikarbadi, is possibly one of the few hotels in India that can boast of its own private airstrip. Not only that, the property houses one of the oldest polo fields and cricket fields of Udaipur, innumerable stables and the equine institute where the famous Marwari horses are bred. Guests staying here are frequently amazed by the tranquillity and peace of this getaway, despite its close proximity to Udaipur, a mere 4 kilometre away. This idyllic retreat was constructed seventy-five years ago as a private royal residence and was converted into a hotel in 1975.

Spectacular Views

The deluxe suites and rooms reflect the hunting lodge's unique outdoorsy character—rugged stone walls, large windows capturing the picturesque mountains and landscaped gardens overflowing with flowering shrubs and trees rarely seen in the region. The family suite with two bedrooms and a private terrace is very art deco. It is furnished with period furniture, old miniature paintings depicting royal hunts and has spectacular views of the Aravali hills and the Deer Park.

Outdoor Pleasures

A dip in the swimming pool makes for the start of a perfect day. The sanctuary is a delight for the adventurous, with horse safaris taking one around the 250-acre sanctuary resort filled with spotted deer, nilgai, long-tailed monkeys, majestic peacocks and migratory birds, and ending the day with a fully laid-out feast deep inside the sanctuary.

As night falls the lights come on at Risala, the open-air restaurant, where the enticing aroma of a barbecue beckons. Shikarbadi also prides itself in serving typical Mewari cuisine and also offers a variety of European style dishes for the less adventurous.

Shikarbadi has something for everyone—from simple riding lessons to safaris, or you can even try your hand at clay-pigeon shooting or polo, the pursuit of many Rajput princes.

Location

Shiv Niwas Palace, a majestic crescent shaped building, located at the southern end of the City Palace complex provides spectacular views of Lake Pichola and the adjacent 'White City' of Udaipur.

Access

Airport: Udaipur – 22 km | **Railway Station:** Udaipur – 2 km | **International Airport:** New Delhi – 664 km

Driving Distance: From Jaipur – 420 km

shiv niwas palace hotel
shimmering crescent

Udaipur, Rajasthan

Tel.: 0294-2528016/19, 2528008 • Email: crs@hrhhotels.com

DYNASTY: Mewar • BUILT: Early 20th-century
STYLE: Mughal and Rajput • CATEGORY: Luxury

Udaipur, the capital of Mewar, was built by Maharana Udai Singh in 1568 and Shiv Niwas Palace was built by his descendant Maharana Bhagwat Singh Mewar in the early 20th-century. Today, it is a grand luxury hotel that takes you back to the era of maharajas and their regal lifestyle.

Even before you reach Shiv Niwas Palace you are overwhelmed by its scale and grandeur. The approach to the imposing palace itself is memorable—a steep climb up a curve brings you to massive wooden gates with pointed iron protrusions aimed directly at anyone wanting to enter the premises without permission.

Imposing Welcome

Once inside, you realize that the palace is much bigger than expected and possibly the grandest of all Rajput palaces. It is not one single palace, actually, but a collection of four separate palaces comprising several wings built by different rulers from the 16th to the 20th century, but well-integrated enough to look like one single palace façade. Here you will find a mix of Mughal decorative and Rajput military architecture: rough-hewn walls, inspiring courtyards, lots of marble, high ceilings, arches and the ubiquitous jharokhas. Even though the exterior walls are bare and unornamented, the interiors are Mewar's tribute to the Mughal durbars—frescoes, coloured glass, decorative pavilions, fountains and lavish use of marble inlay-work.

There was a time when Shiv Niwas Palace was the residence of the maharaja of Mewar, Maharana Fateh Singh, and then it was exclusively reserved for important visiting dignitaries and guests of the royal family (the slightly less important were housed at Laxmi Vilas Palace, some miles away).

'Propah' Treatment

Today, one can book a royal suite, sip champagne in the private balcony or terrace and laze the afternoon away, gazing at the incredibly blue skies over Udaipur. The view of Lake Pichola, walks along the lakefront and romantic candle-lit dinners make one forget that this is the heart of Rajasthan.

At the Shiv Niwas Palace one can experience a truly royal high-tea, served 'so propahly' or a lavish sit-down dinner on the landscaped lawns. The lush-green gardens, glittering lights of the Jagmandir Island and the Lake Palace make the Promenade a unique venue for events. A bagpiper band gives a royal welcome to all guests. Udaipur's other prime tourist attractions—the City Palace Museum and the Old City are only minutes away from Shiv Niwas Palace.

VIP Guests

Illustrious guests who have stayed at Shiv Niwas include King George V in 1905, Queen Elizabeth II, the Duke and Duchess of Kent and Jacqueline Kennedy. It is also a favourite haunt of filmstars, right from Amitabh Bachchan down.

The Mewar festival is celebrated to welcome the advent of spring. It coincides with the festival of Gangaur, which is celebrated in its own inimitable style in Udaipur.

The festival of Gangaur is very important for Rajasthani women. On this special occasion they

wear their best clothes and then gather to dress the image of Isar and Gangaur. The images, resplendent in their finery, are then carried in a ceremonial procession through different parts of the city. The procession winds its way to the Gangaur Ghat at Lake Pichola. Amidst much singing and festivity, they are transferred to special boats. Once the religious ceremony is over, it is time for the cultural events. Songs, dances and other events

Location

The Taj Lake Palace hotel in Udaipur is an exquisite white-marble island palace that seems to float on the still waters of Lake Pichola. Set amid awe-inspiring gardens, this 250-year-old palace is regarded as among the most romantic spots in the world.

Access

Airport: Udaipur – 22 km | **Railway Station:** Udaipur – 2 km | **International Airport:** New Delhi – 664 km

taj lake palace
floating dream

Udaipur, Rajasthan

Tel.: 0294-2428800 • Email: lakepalace.udaipur@tajhotels.com

DYNASTY: Mewar • BUILT: 1746 • RENOVATION: 1963
ARCHITECT (RENOVATION): Garth Sheldon • STYLE: Rajput
CATEGORY: Luxury

Visitors often feel they are seeing a mirage when they catch their first glimpse of the white marble structure of the Lake Palace hotel in the middle of Lake Pichola in the desert city of Udaipur. Originally built as a summer palace for the royal dynasty 250 years ago, against the backdrop of the Aravali hills, the Lake Palace has one of the most scenic locations of any hotel in the world. It was built in 1746 by Maharana Jagat Singh II of Mewar, its courtyards, pavilions and gardens serving as living reminders of a bygone era.

The cool, placid environs and the picture-perfect setting make the Lake Palace an ideal honeymoon destination.

A perfect blend of royal past and the right contemporary flourishes and conveniences, makes a stay here a treat for the discerning traveller.

The temple of Jagannath Rai, now called Jagdishji, is a raised on a tall terrace and was built by Maharana Jagat Singh I in 1651. A double-storied *mandapa* (hall) is attached to a double-storied *saandhara* sanctum (having a covered ambulatory). The *mandapa* has another level tucked within its pyramidal *samavarna* (bell-roof) while the hollow clustered spire over the sanctum contains two more, non-functional levels or stories. Lanes originating from various points along the *sheharpanah* (city wall) converge on the Jagdish Temple and walking through them is a an ideal way to explore the city.

Honeymooner's Haven

The rooms and suites of the Lake Palace offer the prefect ambience for a romantic stay. The royal suites have stained-glass windows, private balconies and traditional ornate *jhoolas* or swings, but with all the creature comforts of the modern age. The views of the lake from any direction are breathtaking and all the interiors have preserved the glorious heritage of the past. Each room and suite is distinctive in its design and captures a different mood and period.

The interiors are in keeping with the standards and style of the erstwhile royal occupants—high ceilings, carved mouldings, ornate glasswork, crystal chandeliers and miniature paintings. Some interiors are embellished with peacock motifs since the peacock is regarded as a symbol of royalty, love, fertility and rain.

There is the Lily Pond courtyard where, in earlier times, Holi—the festival of colour—was celebrated amid singing and dancing, with members of the royal family at the centre of the festivities.

Neel Kamal is the dining restaurant that overlooks the Lily Pond. Reminiscent of royal banquet halls with its gilt embellished arches, it offers local Rajasthani cuisine and other Indian favourites. The Jharokha is the informal all-day dining restaurant by the lake. Its scalloped arches frame splendid views of the lake.

Ceremonial Cruise

There's plenty to do and see in the Lake Palace hotel itself though Udaipur has a plethora of places to visit. Guests can take a cruise in the *Gangaur*, an antique ceremonial barge which recreates the stately splendour of royal cruises. Illuminated by candles and steered by finely-dressed oarsmen, the *Gangaur* glides gently across the lake, giving guests a closer view of the palaces and temples that line its one side.

Rajasthani cooking was influenced by the hardy lifestyle of its inhabitants and the availability of ingredients in this desert region. Scarcity of water and fresh green vegetables has had its effect on the cooking. Dried lentils, beans from indigenous plants like sangri and ker, are liberally used. Gram flour is a major ingredient here and is used to make some of the delicacies like *gatta ki sabzi* and *pakodi*. While *dal*, *bati* and *churma* is the best known food, for the adventurous traveller willing to experiment, there is a lot of variety available.

Location

Offering panoramic views of the Arabian Sea and the Gateway of India, the Taj Mahal Palace & Tower is a Mumbai landmark. Built in 1903, this architectural marvel was India's first luxury hotel bringing together Moorish, Oriental and Florentine styles.

Access

Domestic and International Airport: Mumbai International Airport – 32 km

the taj mahal palace

gateway to india

Mumbai, Maharashtra

Tel.: 022-66653366 • Email: tmhresv.bom@tajhotels.com

OWNERSHIP: Tata Sons • BUILT: 1903
STYLE: Moorish, Oriental and Florentine
CATEGORY: Luxury

The Taj Mahal Palace and Towers, a graceful landmark facing the Gateway of India, is minutes away from the commercial, shopping and banking districts of Mumbai, formerly Bombay.

India's first luxury hotel, the Taj Mahal was built in 1903. 'The Taj Hotel,' noted G.A. Mathews in 1905 'is on such scale of magnificence and luxury that at first it rather took one's breath away.' According to a chronicler of the history of the Taj, it was 'a prince among hotels dotting the British Empire ... it joined the chain of caravanserais which sumptuously punctuated the travel of latter day British imperialists:

For a hotel owned and run by an Indian, the Taj was a pioneer in providing world-class service, style and luxury. This was typical of Jamesetji Tata's many endeavours. He is often credited with single-handedly putting India on the world's industrial map, venturing into areas like steel manufacturing and hydroelectric power generation over a century ago.

Pioneering Luxury

The story goes that the pioneering Parsi industrialist Jamsetji Nusserwanji Tata decided to build the hotel when he was refused entry into a hotel on racial grounds. According to another story, the plague in 1896 convinced Jamsetji that he had to restore the image of his beloved Bombay. Whatever it was, he wanted to build a hotel that would be Indian owned, managed by a European staff and open to visitors and guests of all races.

The hotel's huge reputation rests on the fact that, over the years, it has gone beyond just satisfying the customer's needs. According to a guest, 'This was the most luxurious and service oriented hotel I've ever stayed in. You'll feel like James Bond in an exotic locale as you walk down your ornate Victorian corridor to your elevator! You won't be disappointed

and will be impressed that such levels of luxury and service still exist.'

Architectural Marvel

The hotel is an architectural marvel showcasing contemporary Indian influences along with beautiful vaulted alabaster ceilings, onyx columns, graceful archways, hand-woven silk carpets, crystal chandeliers, a magnificent art collection, an eclectic collection of furniture and a dramatic cantilever stairway. Over the past century, the Taj has amassed a huge collection of paintings and works of art, ranging from Belgian chandeliers to Goan artefacts, becoming a veritable museum.

A large number of galleries run from one end of the edifice to the other and there are a string of verandahs. It was designed in such a way that its entrance is not on the

sea-front but at the back, opening up to the city, so that most of the guests would have rooms overlooking the sea.

Today, the hotel houses fifty generously appointed suites, each decorated with original paintings and period furniture. The heritage rooms are a blend of traditional elegance and modern facilities, and overlook the magnificent Gateway of India and the Arabian Sea. The U-shaped wings of the hotel were specially designed to trap the late afternoon breezes blowing not directly from the harbour but from the Back Bay, thereby ensuring a comfortable stay for the guests.

Famous Guests

Since it has opened in 1903, the Taj has been the haunt of the world's who's who. From maharajas and princes to various kings, presidents, CEOs and entertainers, the Taj has played the perfect host. Its history is also linked with the social and political history of the subcontinent. The Taj was where Nehru, Mohammed Ali Jinnah, Sarojini Naidu and Mahatma Gandhi met to shape India's destiny. Vijaya Raje Scindia, the late Rajmata of Gwalior, met her husband-to-be here and Bill Clinton, former US president stayed at the Taj on his visit to Mumbai a few years ago.

India's Metropolis

Mumbai, it is said, never sleeps. Known as Bombay until 1996, Mumbai is India's commercial capital. Its original name Bombay emerged from the term 'Bom Bahai' meaning a good bay or harbour. The city was formed by the reclamation of seven islands on the central-western coast along the Arabian Sea. Mumbai boomed into a textile city in the 19th century. With the opening up of the Suez Canal in 1869 the city's future as India's primary port was assured. The glamour of a prolific film industry, cricket on weekends, snacking on bhel puri on the Chowpatty beach and red double-decker buses— all this and more add to the city's charm.

A mix of communities and cultures gives the city an aura of vibrancy and vitality that has to be experienced. Mumbai is a melting pot of cultures, something that is reflected in its culinary offerings. One can feast on cuisine from all the states in the country, as well as authentic international cuisine from almost every part of the world.

In and Around Mumbai

Just five kilometres away from the Taj is the busy railway station, Victoria Terminus or VT (now renamed Chattrapati Shivaji Terminus), one of the city's largest buildings built in an elaborate Italian Gothic design. The first train to steam out of this station to nearby Thane was in 1853. Also worth seeing is the Flora Fountain which stands at a busy five-point intersection in the heart of the commercial Fort area.

Ten kilometres to the north of the Gateway of India are the Elephanta Caves. These consist of temples cut into the rock, believed to have been carved between AD 450 and AD 750. The main cave contains large sculpted panels depicting Shiva, and this includes the astonishing six-metre-high triple-headed Trimurti—in which Shiva embodies the roles of the Creator, Preserver and Destroyer.

For those interested in architectural treasures, many of which are now being painstakingly restored, a walk from the Taj Mahal hotel to the Kalaghoda art district is a must. The area, spanning roughly two square kilometres, draws its name from a statue of King Edward VIII astride a black horse (*kala ghoda* in Hindi) that once graced the centre of the main thoroughfare. It is home to restaurants, museums, educational institutions, cultural organizations, theatres and art galleries.

The Gateway of India, opposite the hotel, is a ceremonial arch built in 1927 to commemorate the visit of King George V and Queen Mary. Constructed in honey-coloured basalt, the changing light of the rising and setting sun

Location

With an atmosphere reminiscent of a British club, the Taj West End is a collection of villas and mansions, some of which are over 100 years old. Set amidst twenty acres of magnificent gardens, it is a fine tribute to Bangalore, the garden city of India. Situated opposite the racecourse, Taj West End is a 15-minute drive to the business, entertainment, shopping districts and the golf course.

Access

Airport: Bangalore – 11.5 km | Railway Station: Bangalore – 2 km | International Airport: Bangalore – 11.5 km

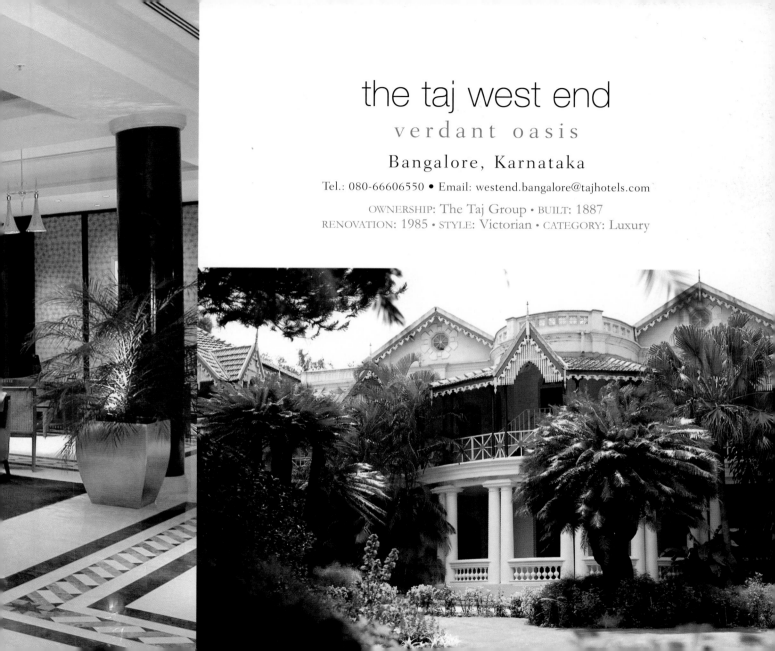

the taj west end

verdant oasis

Bangalore, Karnataka

Tel.: 080-66606550 • Email: westend.bangalore@tajhotels.com

OWNERSHIP: The Taj Group • BUILT: 1887
RENOVATION: 1985 • STYLE: Victorian • CATEGORY: Luxury

Legend has it that King Veeraballa of Vijayanagara once lost his way in forest. Hungry and tired, he came upon a lone hut in the thick forest where he met an old woman. When he asked for food, she gave him baked beans ('Benda Kalu'

Taj West End is Bangalore's unique hotel. Situated near the city centre, the hotel's twenty acres of landscaped gardens are a fine tribute to Bangalore, the garden city of India. The hotel is 10 kilometre (15-minute drive) away from the business, entertainment and shopping districts, and located close to the race course, golf course and the planetarium.

The West End dates back to 1887, when it was a 10-room Victorian boarding house called Bronson's Inn. The Bangalore bungalows were added on later, within the verdant compound, and the current management has retained the property's natural ambience and original architecture.

Colonial Villas

At the Taj West End the rooms and suites are spread across the vast garden acreage; so guest are whisked away to their rooms in a car after check-in. Surrounded by magnificent old banyan trees the villas and mansions that form the accommodation here are a treat. Rooms comprise of various interesting elements such as pitched-roof, verandah blocks and more recent structures modelled on colonial architecture. The private balconies look onto the extensive gardens. Rooms in the Heritage Wing have four-poster beds and old-Bangalore-theme lithographs.

Guests can look forward to a wide selection of cuisines at

in Kannada). This simple fare tasted far better than the rich elaborate meals the king was used to. The king christened this place 'Benda Kalu Ooru' (place of baked beans) to commemorate his satisfying meal!

the in-house restaurants and bar—ranging from casual all-day eateries to formal fine dining. While South Indian delicacies like Idli, Vada and Dosa are a must-have, you can get almost every cuisine from around the world in this cosmopolitan, food-loving city.

In and Around Bangalore

If you've been in India a while, Bangalore, the capital of Karnataka, will probably feel like a long, soothing break from the endless commotion. The first city in India to get electricity, Bangalore continues, in many ways, to blaze the trail in the nation's quest for a modern identity. Bangalore is India's fifth-largest metropolitan city and embodies both history and technology. It has been given several names over the years: at first it was the 'The Garden City of India' then, 'The Neon City' and 'The Pub City of India' and the latest nomenclature is 'India's Silicon Valley'. It is also known as 'Stone City' thanks to its huge granite deposits.

A melting pot of many cultures, the city has developed a vibrant cultural ethos, which absorbs influences from around the country, while preserving the local cultural identity. While in Bangalore try and watch the ancient folk art of Yakshagana or 'Song of the Celestial Beings', an example of the survival of one such tradition.

Location
Situated at the foot of the Dhauladhar Mountains, Taragarh Palace is surrounded by tea gardens in the Kangra valley, one of the most scenic and unexplored areas of Himachal Pradesh.

Access
Airport: Kangra – 53 km, Chandigarh – 270 km | **Railway Station:** Chandigarh – 270 km
International Airport: New Delhi – 520 km | **Driving Distance:** From Shimla – 235 km

taragarh palace

royal escape

Palampur, Himachal Pradesh

Tel.: 01894-242034/243077 • Email: info@taragarh.com

DYNASTY: Dogra • BUILT: 1931 • RENOVATION: 1971
STYLE: Art Deco • CATEGORY: Mid Price

Crescent Moon

Taragarh Palace, set in the picturesque Himalayan forests of Kangra district, was once called Al Hilal or the crescent moon. It was the home of the young Nawab of Bahawalpur who built this large European-style residence in 1931, laying out lush gardens with a glass pleasure-pavilion and a mosque. For the next sixteen years or so, Al Hilal was where he would escape to every summer. But in 1947, India was partitioned and the Nawab decided to leave it all and settle in Pakistan. His grand residence became the property of the Punjab government.

In 1950 it changed hands once again, and was acquired by Maharani Tara Devi of Kashmir who was yearning to spend the last days of her life in Kangra Valley where she had been raised as a young girl. The pleasure pavilion was converted into a temple and the new home was renamed Taragarh. The Maharani moved between her palace in the plains of Jammu, where she spent the winters and Taragarh, where she spent the summer months. In 1971, Karan Singh, Maharani Tara Devi's only son, decided to open this charming private residence to guests and converted it into a hotel.

Breathtaking Panoramas

The old colonial furniture, teak-paneled dining hall and wide verandahs give Taragarh an air of grace and elegance. Sepia tinted photographs and portraits, documenting historic events and personalities depict the glory of princely India. For those who want to experience the outdoors, from October to June there are six fully furnished Swiss tents, with attached bathrooms and running water, designed as camps in the wilderness.

At Taragarh, it is easy to just stay put at the hotel and soak in the beauty of the Himalayan forests and gaze at the snow peaks of the Dhauladhar ranges all day. You can spend the day at the swimming pool, playing tennis or badminton in floodlit courts. Short walks and day-treks with a packed lunch around Taragarh Palace are very popular and for those wanting to explore the place, there are walks through the tea gardens on the slopes of the surrounding hills.

Around Taragarh

A short drive from Taragarh, past Dharamsala, is the residence and headquarters of the Dalai Lama in Mcleodgunj. This hill resort, with the dramatic peaks of the Dhauladhar rising above it, was also very popular with the British. Today, it is a mini, colourful Tibetan township that has the newly-built Gelugpa monastery and a school for Tibetan culture with an excellent library. The little shops sell Tibetan crafts and there are several restaurants that serve Tibetan food. A little higher up the ridge is the pretty church of St. John with beautiful stained-glass windows and the grave of former viceroy, Lord Elgin, in its churchyard.

The Sobha Singh Art Gallery displays original works of Sobha Singh, a Sikh artist who lived here in the 1950s and 60s and later became known for his paintings of the romantic legends of Sohni Mahiwal and Hir Ranjha. And the Andretta Pottery Society nearby specializes in ethnic clay pottery and holds classes for students.

For the adventurous, there is hang-gliding at Billing, 55 kilometre from Taragarh. It is said to be one of the finest sites for hang-gliding in the world. Many international hang-gliding and para-gliding competitions are held here every year.

Location

Umaid Bhawan Palace in Jodhpur is the last of the great palaces of India and one of the largest residences in the world. While very occidental in its symmetrical planning, the palace draws deeply from the Rajput tradition. The building is said to be one of the finest examples of art deco style of architecture in the world.

Access

Airport: Jodhpur – 5 km | **Railway Station:** Jodhpur – 6 km | **International Airport:** New Delhi – 597 km
Driving Distance: From Jaipur – 340 km

umaid bhawan palace
colossal grandeur

Jodhpur, Rajasthan

Tel.: 0291 - 2510101 • Email: ubpresv.jodh@tajhotels.com

DYNASTY: Rathor • BUILT: 1943
ARCHITECT: Henry Lanchester • STYLE: Art Deco
CATEGORY: Mid Price

Royal Visionary

The Rathores of Jodhpur trace their history back to 1459 when Rao Jodha founded the city on the edges of the Thar Desert and made it the capital of the Rathor Kingdom, the largest in Rajputana. Today it is the second largest city in Rajasthan.

The palace was named after Maharaja Umaid Singh, grandfather of the present Maharaja of Jodhpur. A chronicler of Jodhpur's history wrote: 'There was something unique about Maharaja Umaid Singh, an extravagance of vision, similar to that of the Mughals. He, it is believed, enjoyed polo so he took his own team to England with an army of ponies and Jodhpur emerged a world polo power. He loved flying so the Jodhpur Aerodrome became an international airport before Delhi, with three trans-continental airlines stopping here. His decision to dabble in Bombay's fledgling stock market resulted, within a year, in his cornering the shares of the Tata Iron and Steel Company (TISCO), India's first heavy industry. And his famine relief policy, which shames many a modern day development project, changed the very face of Marwar, giving rise to one of the most magnificent royal residences in the world and a dam that remains, half a century later, one of Jodhpur's main sources of drinking water.'

Art Deco Opulence

Umaid Bhawan Palace was designed by the renowned Edwardian architect Henry Lanchester. It is a remarkable blend of eastern and western architectural influences— the Renaissance influenced its majestic 105-foot high cupola, while the towers drew inspiration from the Rajput tradition.

The palatial residence had its own theater, eight dining rooms and a banquet hall which could accommodate upto three hundred people. An oval staircase was flanked on either side by the impressive neo-classical ballroom and the banquet hall. An exclusive smoking room and an elegant wood-paneled library, all conformed to the westernized lifestyle of the modern Rathors, while the throne room, with its exquisite murals from the Indian epic Ramayana, underlined their Indian roots and tradition. There is an indoor swimming pool with a mosaic of zodiac symbols and private garages which house a collection of vintage cars.

If you decide to stay in the Maharani suite, you will be greeted by a mural of the Goddess Kali, etched on shining black glass designed by the self-exiled Polish artist Stefan Norblin. A dressing room with a wardrobe and a bath carved out of a single piece of pink Italian marble are also designed by Norblin. The suite has a large balcony with

In-house Attractions

This splendid palace hotel has two restaurants and a choice of lounges. The private museum is a repository of a rare collection of rocks, watches, fine china, ornate mirrored furniture, glass and crystal ware, and photographs. It also has its own post-office and the well-stocked library is open to the guests.

In and Around Jodhpur

If Jaipur is the Pink City of Rajasthan, Jodhpur is known as the Blue City because of its blue houses. And it is from here that those baggy-tight horse-riding trousers, jodhpurs, took their name. Jodhpur, is one of India's most fascinating cities. One can wander around the streets of the old city or browse through the antique stores or go visit the fort.

Aldous Huxley was spellbound by Jodhpur and the Mehrangarh Fort; he alluded to this desert city in his *Jesting Pilate*. Mehrangarh also impressed the likes of Rudyard Kipling and the renowned architect, Edward Lutyens.

Other than the fort, there are some other interesting places to see in Jodhpur. Jaswant Thada is a cluster of royal cenotaphs in white marble, built in 1899. It also houses the

a spectacular view of the palace gardens and the Mehrangarh Fort. The Maharaja Suite bears murals of leopards from Africa, tigers and horses, and of the famed Jodhpur sport, pig-sticking—all done by Norblin.

portraits of various kings who ruled Jodhpur in the past. Just two kilometres away from the city is the 100-pillared Shiva Temple and five kilometres further north, the 13th-century artificial Bal Samand Lake. The extensive gardens at Mandore have the beautiful *chattris* of Rathor rulers. The 'Hall of Heroes' has fifteen figures carved out of a rock wall and the 'Shrine of 330 million Gods' is painted with figures of deities and spirits. To the southeast of Jodhpur are the Bishnoi villages. The Bishnoi tribes hold all animal life as sacred and the rare blackbuck thrives in this region.

Meherangarh Fort

The Meherangarh Fort at Jodhpur seems to be an organic part of the sheer basalt escarpment it arises from. According to some, the view from the fort of the Old City below is unrivalled anywhere in the world: its alleyways, courtyards and terraces looking like a miniature cityscape painting. Huge gates at the entrance are fitted with iron nails to prevent elephants from bringing them down. The palaces and the mansions within are more delicately designed. The chief palaces you can see in the fort are Phool Mahal, Moti Mahal, Jhanki Mahal, Sheesh Mahal and Sadar Vilas.

Location

Umed Bhawan, one of the most beautiful palaces of Kota in Rajasthan, was built in the prevailing Indo-Saracenic style, subtly blending Rajput and Victorian architecture. Every visiting dignitary, including Queen Mary, who visited Kotah State, as it was known in 1905, has been entertained here.

Access

Airport: Kota – 6 km | **Railway Station:** Kota – 4 km | **International Airport:** New Delhi - 503 km

Driving Distance: From Jaipur – 261 km

umed bhawan palace
picturesque abode

Kota, Rajasthan

Tel.: 0744-2325262 • Email: holidays@welcomheritagehotels.com

DYNASTY: Hada • BUILT: 1905 • ARCHITECT: Swinton Jacob
STYLE: Rajput and Victorian/Indo-Saracenic • CATEGORY: Mid Price

Regal Environs

The Maharaos of Kotah (as Kota was formerly called) had always lived in the medieval fort inside the city, but Maharaja Umed Singh II wanted something more contemporary. He commissioned Sir Swinton Jacob, a distinguished officer of the Royal Engineers in the British Army, to design a new palace for his personal use and the Umed Bhawan came up in 1905. There was generous use of white Khimach and pink sandstone, available in plenty from the nearby quarries, while Italian marble, among other things, was imported for the flooring.

In keeping with the trends of the times, the overall design is in the Indo-Saracenic style. There are several Rajput architectural accents such as parapets, balustrades, arches and decorative brackets—the hallmarks of the Rajput style. Lush lawns and courtyards, picturesque ceilings, marble corridors, hunting trophies of yesteryear along with exquisite royal heirlooms adorn the palace.

In 1930, the palace was enlarged to provide accommodation for Maharaj Kumar Bhim Singh and his bride. George Devon, the designer, took great care to ensure that the new wing blended well with the old. This part of Umed Bhawan remains a private residence while the rest is a hotel.

In and Around Kota

Kota is located on the eastern bank of the Chambal River, Rajasthan's only perennial river. While some associate the place with the famous gossamer thin Kota Doria sarees, made of cotton or silk and embellished with delicate golden thread designs, Kota is also known for the Kota School of miniature paintings, often a vivid and detailed portrayal of hunting expeditions undertaken by the royalty in the once thickly-wooded forests around the place.

Kota is an interesting place to explore and there is plenty to do. For visitors interested in textiles, a visit to Kethun—weaver's village, famous for 'Kota doria' sarees—is a must. Within the city are the City Palace and Fort, Rao Madho Singh Museum, city bazaars, Jag Mandir—one of the most spectacular spots in the city, and the cenotaphs.

Location

Set amidst acres of lush landscaped gardens in the city of Gwalior, is the Usha Kiran Palace. Easily accessible from both the gateway cities of Delhi and Mumbai, this magnificent palace is located next to the exquisite Jai Vilas Palace, the ancestral residence of the Scindia family.

Access

Airport: Gwalior – 14 km | **Railway Station:** Gwalior – 3 km | **International Airport:** New Delhi – 321 km
Driving Distance: From Bhopal – 240 km

usha kiran palace
timeless elegance

Gwalior, Madhya Pradesh

Tel.: 0751-2444000 to 05 • Email: ushakiran.gwalior@tajhotels.com

DYNASTY: Scindias • BUILT: 1885 • RENOVATION: 2004
STYLE: Indo-Saracenic • CATEGORY: Luxury

Less than four hours by express train from Delhi is the Usha Kiran Palace, providing travellers with an excellent base to experience the splendour of Gwalior. Rich in history and with an air of timeless elegance, this 120-year-old palace, which once played host to the King of England, is now a heritage hotel.

Today, the kingdom is no more and the monarchs have become democratically elected representatives of the people, but the splendour of Gwalior lives on in its magnificent palaces, the glittering chandeliers, the exquisitely carved temples and the melodies of the legendary Tansen's ragas.

The spa at Usha Kiran Palace is probably the only spa in the world with live musicians serenading guests with Indian classical music during their treatments. Designed in a minimalist style and themed around the elements of nature, it offers the flavour of royalty and elegance of old India in a new and fresh setting. Old ruins, crumbling structures, trees

Caravanserai

Through centuries, until as late as the coming of the British, the central-Indian state of Madhya Pradesh remained a sort of caravanserai—a resting spot—for travellers, conquerors, mendicants and traders to stop a while, before going further south to the Deccan. Maybe that is why, till John Malcolm wrote his *A Memoir of Central India* in 1824, this state remained a sort of forgotten entity.

As things turned out, it was all for the good. The state never got a star billing in the canvas of Indian history, but then nor was it ever a victim of foreign invasions, needless wars and bloodshed. The rugged ramparts of Gwalior reverberate with tales of the past which can be traced back to the 6th century. One such tale recounts how the patron saint of the shepherds and cowherds, Gwalipa, cured the king, and thus the city was named Gwalior after him.

Enduring Elegance

The romance and legend of Gwalior, with its warriors, kings and poets, lives on even though the kingdom is no longer extant.

Usha Kiran Palace was named after the daughter of the late Maharaja Jiwaji Rao Scindia. Its architecture is in keeping with the true Gwalior tradition; the palace has a corridor enclosed on one side by exquisitely filigreed stone screens. The palace compound has abundant fruit and flowering trees, sprawling lawns, arched bridges and a sparkling fountain with coloured lights.

Class and Comfort

The elegantly styled rooms reflect the local culture and architecture. Light, airy and modern, each room is unique, offering gorgeous views and décor befitting royalty. The rooms are lavishly furnished with divans, silk cushions and gossamer-thin silk curtains edged with gold.

The Chand Nivas and Suraj Nivas, the two luxury suites, are adorned with ornate, coloured light-fixtures, Venetian mirrors and mother-of-pearl mosaics. Each has a canopied bed, a massage bed, lounge area and water fountains, and commands a magnificent view of the grand Gwalior Fort.

and swings, along with the two stone lions standing guard at the beautiful pool, add to its appeal. Located in the palace gardens, it has treatment suites, a meditation garden with fruit bearing trees cocooned within ancient pillars and an open heritage courtyard.

In Gwalior

While at Usha Kiran Palace, a must-see is the adjoining Jai Vilas Palace. Built by Maharaja Jayaji Rao Scindia, the palace is still occupied by the Scindia family. This Victorian Gothic structure houses two of the world's largest crystal chandeliers, the famous silver train that used to serve royal guests during banquets and Asia's largest and most exquisite one-piece carpet woven by a hundred craftsmen over twelve years.

There is the massive Gwalior Fort, a 1,000-year-old fortress which rises on a hill near the infamous Chambal ravines. Then there is the Man Mandir Palace, the Gujari Mahal and the quaint ninth-century 'Saas Bahu' temples apparently built for a mother and daughter-in-law who prayed separately as they worshipped two different gods.

Location
Rising like a dream in the Sahyadri Ranges, Matheran, Asia's only pedestrian hill resort, is just 120 kilometres away from Mumbai.

Access
Airport: Mumbai – 120 km | **Railway Station:** Neral – 21 km | **International Airport:** Mumbai – 120 km
Driving Distance: From Mumbai – 120 km

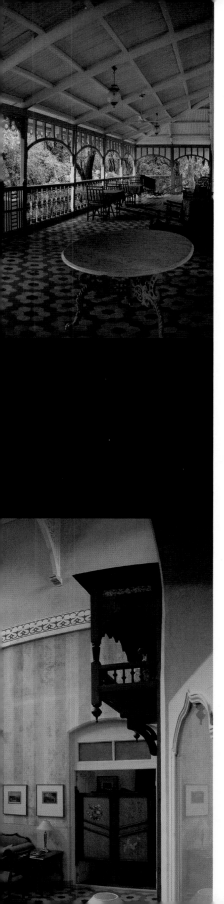

the verandah in the forest
nostalgia among the hills
Matheran, Maharashtra

Tel.: 02148-230296/230810 • Email: sales@neemranahotels.com

OWNERSHIP: Neemrana Group • BUILT: 19th century • RENOVATION: 2001
ARCHITECT (RENOVATION): Kirti Unwalla and Francis Wacziarg
STYLE: Colonial • CATEGORY: Mid Price

By the 19th century the British Empire had a strong foothold in the subcontinent, but there was one thing they just could not come to terms with—the heat. Whether they were stationed in Delhi, Calcutta or Bombay, they were always on the lookout for higher altitudes where they could escape to during the oppressively hot months. So, they built houses in the hills of Shimla near Delhi, in Darjeeling near Calcutta, Ooty in the South, and Matheran near Bombay (now Mumbai).

Shivaji's Ladder

Matheran was 'discovered' by an English officer, Hugh Malet, in 1870, while he was climbing a path called Shivaji's ladder, as that was the route taken by Shivaji, the great 17th-century Maratha warrior-king, whenever he needed to make a quick getaway.

Today, many Mumbaikars (as the people from Bombay are known) come to Matheran, to take a quick break from the hectic pace of the city. You can drive down from Mumbai to Dasturi where you park your car or chug up in a toy train. Then you either walk, trot on a horse, or sit in a palanquin, as they did in the years gone by, and go past the gigantic mansions built by the British, the Parsis and the Bohras till you reach the town centre.

Easy Languor

The town is choc-a-bloc with hotels and mansions turned into guesthouses; among the most charming is the Verandah, which is steeped in Raj nostalgia and, given its British and Parsi history, the most atmospheric.

Here you can lounge in a verandah or read under the highest domestic ceiling you would have seen. The Dubash Hall, a neutrally coloured front-room with high ceilings, has a great selection of coffee-table books. A three-course meal is served in the connecting room, Malet Hall, on a candle-laden dining table which seats at least two dozen guests at one time.

Around Matheran

One can stroll down to Charlotte Lake, relish the local cuisines, watch the spectacular sunrise from a vantage point or just let their mind wander, and soak in the peace and quiet. This hill station, situated at an altitude of 800 metre, has many trails that zigzag up the hillside and encircle the hilltop, making it an excellent trekking destination.

Location

Situated on the Observatory Hill in Darjeeling, West Bengal, the Windamere hotel overlooks the town's main promenade and is a reminder of the lifestyle of colonial planters. From here you can get a magnificent view of the Himalayas and the frontiers of Tibet, Bhutan, Nepal and Sikkim.

Access

Airport: Bagdogra - 90 km | **Railway Station:** Darjeeling – 0.5 km | **International Airport:** Kolkata - 690 km

the windamere
glorious panoramas
Darjeeling, West Bengal

Tel.: 0354-2254041/42 • Email: reservations@windamerehotel.net, windamere@windamerehotel.net

OWNERSHIP: Welcome Heritage Group • DATE OF CONSTRUCTION: 1889
RENOVATION: 1939 • STYLE: Colonial • CATEGORY: Luxury

Whenever someone mentions Darjeeling in India, the hill-town in the northeastern part of the country, three things come immediately to mind: tea, the toy train and the Windamere.

Planter's Boarding House

It's a wonder that the Windamere survives and remains to this day one of the most original heritage hotels in India. The credit for this must go to the Tenduf la family who not only own the hotel but have run it since the days of the Raj, when the officialdom moved in one great swelling tide to this town, built on narrow mountain ridges, to escape from the sweltering heat of the plains.

The Windamere started in 1889 as a nondescript boarding house for English and Scottish bachelor tea-planters, with a rather prosaic name Ada Villa. In 1939, it metamorphosed into one of the country's best hotels and attracted many travellers from around the world, hosting many famous names from India and overseas. The guest-book lists comments from the likes of Begum Aga Khan in 1945; Albert, King of Belgium and his queen, Elizabeth in September 1925; Lord Lytton; Lord Reading; C. Rajagopalchari and Sir Edmund Hillary, to name just a few.

The King and the American

There is one particular story which still causes a romantic flutter among guests, more than two decades after it happened. It is, of course, the story of Hope Cook and the King of Sikkim, when the cozy drawing room of the Windamere hotel became the setting of a royal romance. Hope Cook, an American visiting Darjeeling, met her future husband, the then King of Sikkim. But not all the guests have been famous or glamourous.

Life magazine once wrote: 'The Windamere is a sort of place tourists search for in Britain. Often vainly. It is so chintzy and so cosy. It provides a hot water bottle for each foot, and its guests tend to chat with other...' The famous travel writer, Jan Morris found the town and the hotel equally entrancing and endowed both with a contemporary immortality in her widely read book, *Among the Cites*.

Memories of the Raj

A stay at the Windamere is full of Raj nostalgia—oriental rugs worn thin, the wind-up phonograph playing the same music it played in 1920, high tea in the drawing room with trays of sandwiches and sweets laid out on the mahogany buffet, the worn and rickety furniture, long-stay guests slumped back on faded settees talking of books and plays, and arguing over marmalade brands.

The hotel consists of two wings. The first, The Windamere, is furnished in the traditional colonial style with flowered chintz curtains and no television or telephone in the room. It is therefore meant exclusively for those who wish to get away from city life. This wing includes a honeymoon cottage, House of the Eighth Happiness, and Little Peppers, which is also very popular. Little Windamere, on the other hand, has modern facilities and décor.

Darjeeling and Around

Places to see while in Darjeeling include: Tenzing Rock, the famous Darjeeling tea estates, Chourasta—the town's main square, Sunday market, Observatory Hill, Ghoom and Bhotia Bustee Monasteries, Tiger Hill which is 11 kilometre from Darjeeling and the Lloyd Botanical Gardens.

Location

Nestled deep in a dense pine forest in the hills of Shimla, the Woodville Palace retains all the flavours of the Raj era. It can be reached by road from Delhi, via Chandigarh and Kalka, but the most charming journey is from Kalka to Shimla in the toy train.

Access

Airport: Jubarhatti – 20 km | **Railway Station:** Shimla – 7 km | **International Airport:** New Delhi – 385 km

woodville palace
pine forest retreat
Shimla, Himachal Pradesh

Tel.: 0177-2623919/2624038 • Email: woodvillepalacehotel@yahoo.com

DYNASTY: Rathor • BUILT: 1865
RENOVATION: 1938 • STYLE: Art Deco • CATEGORY: Luxury

Shimla, once the summer capital of the British Raj and now a state capital and a bustling town, still has some preserved corners that remind one of the days gone by—Woodville Palace is one of them.

Old-World Charm

This charming estate dates back to 1865 when Sir William Mansfield, Commander in Chief of the Imperial Army became its first resident. Almost 150 years later, Woodville retains the old-world charm of wood and stone structures with plenty of lush foliage and greenery.

Raja Rana of Jubbal, who had a penchant for detail, reconstructed the Woodville building in 1938. He had hundreds of expert artisans brought in from as far as China to ensure the highest quality of craftsmanship. Immaculate gardens with a big, green lawn, a rarity in the hills, skirt the building which has many glass windows with spectacular views of the Himalayas; there is ivy growing up to the first level of the building. Kanwar Uday Singh, the grandson of Raja Rana, opened a part of the mansion as a guesthouse in 1977.

Shimla and Around

Situated at an altitude of 7,000 feet, Shimla was once a nondescript village. It became popular with the British in the 1830s and later became the summer capital of the Imperial government. Enticed by its salubrious character, the British spent more time at this 'hill station' than at the real capital, which was then in Calcutta. Today, it is the state capital of Himachal Pradesh and retains some of the flavour of the Raj. While the location of the estate lends itself perfectly as a base from where one can go trekking, other activities that can be engaged in are riding, golfing, skating and fishing.

Other Heritage Hotels

AJIT BHAWAN
Circuit House
Jodhpur
Rajasthan-342006

HOTEL BHADRAWATI PALACE
Bhandarej
Distt. Dausa
Rajasthan-303501

BIJAY NIWAS PALACE RESORT
V.P.O. Badi, Bijay Nagar
Ajmer
Rajasthan-305001

BISSAU PALACE
Outside Chandpole
Near Saroj Cinema, Jaipur
Rajasthan-302016

BRIJRAJ BHAWAN PALACE
Civil Lines, Kota
Rajasthan-324001

HOTEL CARAVANSERAI
14 Lalghat, Udaipur
Rajasthan-313001

CASTLE AWAN
Tehsil Deoli, P.O. Awan
Via Duni, Distt. Tonk
Rajasthan

HOTEL CASTLE BIJAIPUR
V.P.O. Bijaipur
Distt. Chittorgarh
Rajasthan-312001

CAMA RAJPUTANA CLUB RESORT
Adherdevi Road, Mt. Abu
Rajasthan-307501

CASTLE DURJAN NIWAS
P.O. Daspan
Distt. Jalore
Rajasthan-343029

CHANDRAMAHAL HAVELI
Peharsar-Jaipur-Agra Road
Nadbal Tehsil, Distt. Bharatpur
Rajasthan

CHAPSLEE
Lakkar Bazar
Shimla
Himachal Pradesh-171001

HOTEL CHEVRON FAIRHAVENS
Adjacent to Head P.O. Mallital
Nainital
Uttaranchal-263001

CHIRMI PALACE HOTEL
Dhuleshwar Garden
C-scheme, SP Road, Jaipur
Rajasthan-302001

CONNAUGHT HOUSE
Rajendra Marg
Mount Abu
Rajasthan-307501

DEOGARH MAHAL
Madarja
Distt. Rajsamand
Rajasthan-313331

DUNDLOD FORT
Dundlod Fort Pvt. Ltd
Dundlod
Rajasthan-333702

FORT CHANWA
Village Luni
Distt. Jodhpur
Rajasthan

FORT DHARIYAWAD
P.O. Dhariyawad
Distt. Udaipur
Rajasthan-313001

THE FORT NALAGARH
Solan
Himachal Pradesh-174101

THE FORT UNIARA
Gardh Uniara, Uniara
Distt. Tonk
Rajasthan- 304024

GOLDEN CASTLE RESORT
Village Pachar
Distt. Sikar
Rajasthan-332729

GRACE COTTAGE
558, Old Chari Road
Kotwali Bazzar, Dharmsala
Himachal Pradesh-176215

HARI NIWAS PALACE HOTEL
Palace Road,
Jammu (Tawi)
Jammu & Kashmir-180001

HARI MAHAL PALACE
Achrol House
Civil Lines, Jaipur
Rajasthan

THE HOUSE OF MANGALDAS
Opp. Sidi Saiyad Mosque
Lal Darwaja, Ahmedabad
Gujarat - 380001

JAGRAM DURG
P.O. Nimaj
Distt. Pali
Rajasthan-306303

JAWAHAR NIWAS PALACE
No.1 Bada Bagh Road,
P.O Box No.1, Jaisalmer
Rajasthan-345001

JEHAN NUMA PALACE
Jehan Numa Palace Hotel Pvt. Ltd.
157, Shamla Hill, Bhopal-13
Madhya Pradesh

JHALAMANDGARH
P.O. Jhalamand
Distt. Jodhpur
Rajasthan-342005

JHIRA BAGH PALACE
Mandu Road
Dhar
Madhya Pradesh-454001

KARNI KOT
Sodawas, C/O Hotel Karni Bhawan
Palace Road Jodhpur
Rajasthan-342006

KASMANDA PALACE
The Mall Road
Mussoorie
Uttar Pradesh-248179

KESAR BHAWAN PALACE
Mt. Abu
Rajasthan-307501

KOTRI RAOLA
Post & Village Kotri
Distt. Pali
Rajasthan

LAKSHMI VILAS PALACE
Kakaji Ki Kothi
Bharatpur
Rajasthan-321001

LAL NIWAS
Dadha's Mohalla
Phalodi
Rajasthan-342301

LAXMI VILAS PALACE
Opp. Fateh Sagar Lake
Udaipur
Rajasthan-313004

MAHARANI BAGH ORCHARD RETREAT
Sardari, Near Ranakpur Temples
Distt. Pali
Rajasthan-306702

MANDIR PALACE
Gandhi Chowk
Jaisalmer
Rajasthan-345001

THE MUD FORT
Village Kuchesar
Via BB Nagar
Distt. Bulandshahr, UP

MUKUNDGARH FORT
Distt. Jhunjhunu
Rajasthan-333705

NARAIN NIWAS PALACE HOTEL
Kanota Bagh, Narain Singh Road
Jaipur
Rajasthan-302004

NARAYAN NIWAS PALACE
Malka Prol, Jaisalmer
Rajasthan-345001

NILAMBAG PALACE HOTEL
Distt. Bhavnagar
Gujarat-364002

ORCHHA PALACE
Orchha, Distt. Tikamgarh
Madhya Pradesh

PACHEWARGARH
Pachewar, Via Malpura
Distt. Tonk
Rajasthan-304509

THE PALACE
Wankaner
Gujarat-363621

PALACE HOTEL
Bikaner House
Delwara Road, Mount Abu
Rajasthan-307501

THE PALACE UTELIA
Utelia
Distt. Ahmedabad
Gujarat-382230

PALKIYA HAVELI
Mokha, Near Suraj Pole
Kota
Rajasthan

RAHEEM RESIDENCY
Beach Road
Alleppey
Kerala-688012

THE RAJ PALACE
Outside Jorawer Singh Gate,
Amer Road, Jaipur
Rajasthan-302002

RAJMAHAL BHINDAR
P.O. Bhindar
Distt. Udaipur
Rajasthan-313603

RAJMAHAL PALACE HOTEL
Sardar Patel Marg
C-Scheme, Jaipur
Rajasthan-302001

RAMGARH LODGE
Ramgarh Lake
Jaipur
Rajasthan-303109

RANG NIWAS PALACE
Lake Palace Road, Udaipur
Rajasthan-313001

RANJIT'S SVAASA
47-A Mall Road
Amritsar
Punjab-143001

RAWLA NARLAI
Village Narlai, via Desuri
Distt. Pali
Rajasthan

REGENCY VILLA PALACE
Fernhill Palace
Fernhill Post
Ootacamund-643004

ROHET GARH
P.O. Rohet
Distt. Pali
Rajasthan-346421

ROOP NIWAS PALACE
Nawalgarh
Distt. Jhunjhunu
Rajasthan

ROYAL CASTLE GHANERAO
Ghanerao
Distt. Pali
Rajasthan-306704

ROYAL CASTLE KANOTA
Village & P.O. Kanota
Distt. Jaipur
Rajasthan-302004

ROYAL RAJWADA
Bhadrajun
Distt. Jalore
Rajasthan-307031

THE ROYAL RETREAT
Shivpati Nagar
Distt. Siddharth Nagar
Uttar Pradesh-272206

SAMODE HAVELI
Gangapole
Jaipur
Rajasthan-302002

SARDAR SAMAND PALACE
Sardar Samand
Distt. Pali
Rajasthan-306103

SARISKA PALACE
Sariska
Distt. Alwar
Rajasthan-301022

THE SAWAI MADHOPUR LODGE
Ranthambore Road
Sawai Madhopur
Rajasthan

SHAHPURA GARDEN PALACE
N.H.8, Shahpura
Distt. Jaipur
Rajasthan-303103

SHEIKHPURA KOTHI
Hansi
Distt. Hissar
Haryana-122002

SPRINGFIELD
Shimla
Himachal Pradesh

STERLING SWAMIMALAI
56, 4th Street
Abiramapuram, Chennai
Tamil Nadu-600018

SUKDHAM KOTHI
Civil Lines, Kota
Rajasthan-324001

SURYA SAMUDRA BEACH GARDEN
Pulinkudi, P.O. Mullur
Thiruvananthapuram
Kerala-695521

UDAI BILAS PALACE
Dungarpur
Rajasthan-314001

VILLA POTTIPATI
142, 8th Cross, 4th Main Road,
Malleswaram, Bangalore
Karnataka-560003

ISBN: 978-81-7436-389-3

© Roli Books Pvt. Ltd., 2012
Third impression
Published in India by Roli Books
M-75, Greater Kailash-II Market
New Delhi - 110 048, India.
Ph.: ++91-11-4068 2000
Fax: ++91-11-29217185
Email: info@rolibooks.com
Website: www.rolibooks.com

Editor: Himanshu Bhagat
Design: Sneha Pamneja
Layout: Naresh L. Mondal

Printed and bound at Replika Press, India.